4⁰⁰

ch liv

THE
JUSTICE
REVOLUTION

A Biblical Response
to Global Injustice

W9-CYA-992

BARRY SULLIVAN

LIGHT FORCE PUBLISHING

2310 Leonard Drive • Seffner, FL 33584
www.OperationLightForce.com

The Justice Revolution

© 2012, Barry Sullivan

Lightforce Publishing
operationlightforce@gmail.com

Barry Sullivan, Author
barry@thejusticerevolution.com

ISBN 978-0-9778666-1-8

Cover design by Barry Sullivan

Layout design by Barry Sullivan

Author's photo by Brandee Rissmiller

ISAIAH 58:5-10

Is this the kind of fast I have chosen,
only a day for a man to HUMBLE himself?
Is it only for bowing one's head like a reed
and for lying on sackcloth and ashes?
Is that what you call a fast,
a day ACCEPTABLE to the LORD?

Is not this the kind of fasting I have chosen:
to LOOSE the chains of INJUSTICE
and untie the cords of the yoke,
to set the oppressed free
and BREAK every yoke?

Is it not to SHARE your food with the HUNGRY
and to provide the poor wanderer with shelter—
when you see the NAKED, to clothe him,
and not to turn away from your own flesh and blood?

Then your LIGHT will break forth like the dawn,
and your healing will quickly appear;
then your RIGHTEOUSNESS will go before you,
and the GLORY of the LORD will be your rear guard.

Then you will call, and the LORD will ANSWER;
you will CRY for help, and he will say: Here am I.
If you do away with the yoke of OPPRESSION,
with the pointing finger and malicious talk,

and if you SPEND yourselves in behalf of the HUNGRY
and satisfy the NEEDS of the oppressed,
then your light will rise in the darkness,
and your night WILL become like the noonday.

ABOUT THE AUTHOR

Barry and his wife Tracy have been called to awaken a silent and sleeping generation. It is their heart to see this generation come into their full identity as Sons and Daughters of God, and the Sullivan's time in ministry has always reflected that. After a decade as youth pastors they stepped into a different role after starting and then pastoring their own church for six years in the Tampa Bay area. Then in 2007, they felt the Lord calling them back to a full-time youth focus "because they need Fathers to lead them". Within a few months they had merged their church in with another local congregation and started Mahaneh Dan Ministries, having a focus on gathering and equipping youth from around the community to impact their world for Christ.

Barry has also spent time on the mission field, ministering in nations in Central and South America and the Caribbean, and he lived in Paraguay for a year as a young man, helping to start what is now a thriving church in a rural community. More recently he traveled the country stirring youth groups to evangelism as the director of The 40 Day Revolution with Operation Light Force.

Barry and Tracy currently live with their four sons in the Tampa Bay area where they support local congregations through worship, and serve as their city's National Day of Prayer coordinators.

Barry can be contacted at barry@thejusticerevolution.com

DEDICATIONS

To my sons Andrew, Caleb, Josiah, Noah, and all your brothers and sisters of your generation... May you be awakened to what God is doing in the times you live in and never fall asleep again.

And to my wife Tracy... for teaching me the reality of Paul's challenge in Hebrews 12:1-2, and for fixing your eyes on Jesus every time. Thank you for pushing for *Justice* even when I wasn't listening.

I love each of you dearly.

ACKNOWLEDGEMENTS

There are many who need to be thanked for their help and encouragement along the way. First, my mother, who has lived out a life of intercession in front of me. My good friend Richard Mull of Operation Light Force, who believed in and supported this book from the beginning. John and Michelle Skorski, for your years of faithful service to ignite a fire in the emerging generations and for challenging a camp full of youth to cry out to the Father for Justice, which provided the initial inspiration for this book. Sue Salles of Richest of Fare, your help and input with the abortion issue was invaluable – and yours is still the best challenge I've heard on the subject. Pastor Brian and Sister Kimm, thank you for faithfully loving our family as this book was birthed. To all of the friends who said yes to reading the manuscript when it was a work in progress, thank you for your insight and ideas along the way. A special thanks to Cana Bamberg, a teen who said yes to reading the manuscript, then floored me when she also actually did all the assignments – you're quite an inspiration at only 14 years old! And to all men and women who are right now tirelessly working in the seven causes that I address in this book... may you always have what you need in order to do what God has called you to do. My prayer is that this book brings a fresh Wind and fresh troops to support you in your work.

FORWARD

The book you are holding in your hand WILL change you and your life if you let it. I believe that it cannot help but change your life. It has changed me and my life, and it has changed how I think and what I do.

I read *The Justice Revolution* completely through before doing the things it asked me to do. It was a daily journey but I wanted to know what lay ahead each day, so I picked it up one night and could not put it down. Now I am actually doing it with more than 20 college aged young adults. They are so excited and impacted even though the things they are being asked to do are not easy. One day they ate nothing but rice all day. They hated the rice, but they loved the experience. This Friday we will sleep all night in cardboard boxes on a busy street in our town, and the students can't wait.

We are giving up our favorite things like not watching TV and not getting on Facebook. We are giving up so many things we normally love, and everyone is excited about it and enjoying it.

I know this may not make any sense!

Our comfort levels and easy lives have actually lulled us into a stupor that we don't realize we are in. Getting outside of our comfort zone is actually helping us realize that the things we love have become idols that steal from us our time and real joy.

Eternal values are capturing our minds and hearts.

Have you lost perspective on what really matters? Do you think and do little about the things that are foremost on the heart of God? God cares for the homeless, widows, orphans and the oppressed. He is calling His people to love, to action, to sharing His love with a lost world, but WE ARE TOO BUSY.

You are too busy to do this book. I know it. So was I. It is very inconvenient. If you are looking for convenience, this is not for you. If you want more comfort and separation from the real issues of our day, this book is not for you.

If, however, you want to really know the things God is looking at and calling His people to do, then this book is for you. You will be changed. You will be informed, and you will have to act. If all you do is read this book, then it won't impact you. Your head will have some new information in it but your heart won't be changed.

This is not a 21 day revolution. It is a life-time revolution if you will let it be.

Richard Mull

INTRODUCTION

In January of 1999 a small group of youth pastors were gathered together in a hotel meeting space in Tampa, Florida. We were challenged to see what could happen when youth groups from around our community would join together for an extended period of time, challenging our teens to show the love of God in practical ways by blessing, serving and praying for their friends, classmates, teachers and administrators. Out of that meeting an evangelism strategy called **"The 40 Day Revolution"** was born.

In the decade since that meeting I have had the privilege to be a part of the ministry that helped over 1 million world-wide accept the Revolution challenge. Tens of thousands have been brought into the Kingdom of God as schools, churches and neighborhoods have been turned upside down by young people passionately desiring to share God's love with the world around them. **However, the passion cannot stop there.** The Gospel message doesn't stop at salvation – it confronts the very heart of the evil that causes so many injustices in this world. The example that Christ set for us on the cross truly is that there is no greater love that we could have for mankind than to unselfishly lay our lives down on its behalf. If we truly want to see the world transformed around us, we have to be willing to get involved in ways we never thought before. We have to be willing to get **EXTREME**.

"The Justice Revolution" is my response to injustices that plague the world today... things like poverty, slavery, sex-trafficking and the plight of the child-soldiers of the world. I believe that if the Body of Christ were not only **awakened** to the magnitude of what is taking place in the world around us, but were **compelled to get involved** in a stronger way, then we could truly have an impact and see radical change take place... spiritually, socially and politically.

Will you take this journey with me? Are you ready for another Revolution?

Committed to the Cause,

Barry Sullivan
March 31st, 2009

WARNING:

Something you need to understand right from the start is that **"The Justice Revolution"** is not just another nice youth group curriculum or Bible study to go through with your friends. And no, it's not a comfortable devotional that you can just put back on your shelf when done. It will **open your eyes** with the reality of what is going on around the world, and **challenge you** to change your way of thinking. It will pull you out of your "Thursday night 'American Idol' comfort zone" and **confront you** with the horrors that young people your age and younger go through every day around the world. And it will challenge you to get personally involved. **DO YOU STILL WANT TO GET EXTREME?**

Over the next 21 days you will be introduced to 7 different "social injustices" and challenged to make sacrifices... to do some pretty uncomfortable things... to draw attention to yourself, and in turn draw attention to that day's injustice. You will stand out, be talked about, laughed at, pointed at and misunderstood. **DO YOU STILL WANT TO GET EXTREME?**

"THE JUSTICE REVOLUTION" STRATEGY

INFORM Each day you will be introduced to a "social injustice" – that is when not all people within a society have equal access to the facilities, services or systems within that society, and when people are less fairly treated than others due to their ethnicity, age, gender or religion.

ACT! After you've been given some understanding about that injustice, then you will be challenged to DO something that makes it "hit home." This is where it gets difficult... but you CAN do it!

DEBRIEF It is easy to get caught up in the activism and politics of an injustice and forget that the root of it all is selfishness and sin. That is why each day you will also be brought to God's Word to get you thinking about what it is God is saying to you about that day's focus, and what you can do in your life to affect change concerning that injustice.

PRAY Each day you will be given a prayer focus tied to that day's injustice. If we do anything apart from the presence of God, it is just works. Prayer invites God into the process and empowers our work.

THE CAUSES:

These are the seven "justice causes" that you will focus on over the next 21 days. Each cause will be touched on 3 different times, with a different focus each time.

POVERTY

At least 80% of humanity lives on less than $10 a day.

THE PERSECUTED CHURCH

Every day more than 2 million Christians worldwide suffer for their faith.

HUMAN TRAFFICKING & EXPLOITATION

If you think slavery ended with abolition 150 yrs ago, you're wrong.

ABORTION

Worldwide, one baby is aborted every two seconds.

ACCESS TO CLEAN WATER

The water and sanitation crisis claims more lives through disease than any war claims through guns.

CHILD SOLDIERS AROUND THE WORLD

Right now globally there are as many as 300,000 children serving as soldiers for both rebel groups and government forces in armed conflict.

HOMELESSNESS

Each year in the US alone, more than 2 million teens experience an episode of homelessness.

COMMITMENT PAGE

What you are about to do IS going to be hard. I am asking a lot of you… a sacrifice of time, comfort, and convenience. But I am convinced that if you commit yourself to this, that you WILL walk away changed.

Take a moment right now and consider this. If you are ready for your eyes to opened – for your view of your community and the world to be changed, and to begin to see things the way that God sees them – then read the statements below out loud and commit yourself to joining this Justice Revolution.

As I go through *The Justice Revolution* over the next 21 days:

1. I commit to pray and ask God each day to give me His eyes and ears for that day's injustice, to gain His heart for the world.

2. I commit to taking the time to look at the Scriptures listed out each day so that I can see these issues as God sees them.

3. I commit to doing each day's assignment to the best of my ability so that I will gain an understanding of those who suffer in the world.

By signing below I commit myself to this Cause.

_____   _____

Signature   Date

(This is not a legal document that ties you to The Justice Revolution, rather a symbolic gesture created for your encouragement.)

A Biblical Response to Global Injustice

An act of *justice* is an act of intervention for the helpless – an act of defense for those who are too weak to defend themselves.

INSPIRE

WEEK ONE: ARE YOU AWAKE?

"One of the great liabilities of life is that all too many people find themselves living amid a great period of social change, and yet they fail to develop the new attitudes, the new mental responses, that the new situation demands. They end up sleeping through a revolution." - *Martin Luther King, Jr from a sermon he delivered at the National Cathedral, Washington D.C., on March 31st, 1968.*

Dr. King was referring to the story *Rip Van Winkle* as he spoke that day before a packed church. In this folk tale, Rip is a lazy but kind mountain man living in the days of Colonial America, who goes on a walk up a mountain to escape the complaints of his wife. While there he comes across a strange celebration that he joins in on, and then promptly lays down to take a nap – only to wake up some 20 years later! When he went up the mountain, he passed a sign that had a large picture of King George of England on it… and when he came down, the picture was now that of George Washington, first president of the newly formed United States. In his laziness and desire to escape confrontation, Rip had allowed himself to sleep through a revolution.

My prayer for those of you reading and taking part in this challenge is that God would awaken you to the revolution that has been stirred in our generation. We are at such a place in history as Rip was, where there is great need for social, moral, and spiritual change. It will take courage and commitment to stand against the spirit of apathy and materialism that marks your generation… but I for one believe that you are up to the task. It isn't time to head for the hills to avoid confrontation. No, the Revolution is raging – are you awake?

Day 1 - Sunday

CHILD SOLDIERS AROUND THE WORLD

"If you die, white man, your people will cry because they have their freedom. But for me if I die, our people can't cry, because too many people have died... I have lost 5 brothers in the war."

A CHILD SOLDIER, Sudan

INFORM

What images flash into your mind when you think of war? Do you picture tanks rumbling through open battle fields or through the streets of ruined cities? Rows of soldiers marching in step? The truth is that most armed conflicts in the world today are fought with small arms, and many of the soldiers involved are children under the age of 18. Right now there are more than half a million children who are part of armies in more than 85 countries, with more than 300,000 of them fighting in active conflict!

One country that has had the eyes of the world on it for quite a while is Uganda. For almost 30 years the government has been at war with the "Lord's Resistance Army," a rebel group led by a self-proclaimed messiah figure named Joseph Kony. He has literally brought a country to its knees through the use of fear and has masacred or displaced tens of thousands, while literally kidnapping more than 30,000 children and forcing them to serve in his army or as sex slaves. For years, thousands of children would flee their villages at night and do anything they could to avoid being taken by Kony's group. These children came to be known as "night walkers".

It was after visiting the area and seeing those children that three young American men decided to make a film in 2003 to share the tragedy and story of what was taking place in the area. That film was called "Invisible Children", and it created a groundswell of activism in young people literally all over the world. Seeing that movie at a youth camp one summer is what caused me to start looking at the injustices of the world, and one of the reasons that I wrote this book.

ACT Imagine being the parent of one of these children. You are asleep in your home, and in the middle of the night you awaken to the sound of angry shouts and gunfire in your village. Armed soldiers - children, teens and adults - come into your home and steal your children from you. Then they take them far away into the jungle, desensitize them, and train them to be ruthless killers. They take away what is most valuable to you, and there is nothing you can do.

ASSIGNMENT: *Give it Up!* Today you are going to surrender that thing that you consider most valuable to you. Is it your cell phone? Your Xbox? Maybe it's an IPod, make-up, or even your car. Well, you are about to give it up for the next 21 days to see just a taste of what it feels like to have something you care about taken away from you. You will need to turn this over to someone you trust. Ask that person to put it someplace where you can't get to it. The next thing is that over the next 3 weeks, we want you to start collecting spare change in a "rescue" jar. At the end of this time you'll get the chance to "buy back" whatever it is that's been taken from you today. Get your friends, family, and coworkers involved in chipping in, because it will go to a good cause.

Now, how does this make you feel? When you compare what YOU are giving up today with what those parents have given up, what comes to your mind?

_____
_____
_____
_____
_____
_____

PRAY: That Joseph Kony would be captured and surrender his life to Christ, and that God would bring to light and expose the plans of men like him around the globe.

DAY 1: CHILD SOLDIERS AROUND THE WORLD 1

DEBRiEF If there is something that rises up inside of you when you hear of the horrors that just one man like Joseph Kony has done, imagine how those actions offend the heart of God. I want you to not just learn about these injustices or simply do something unusual to get you thinking about them – no, over the next 21 days I want you to see what God's Word says about them. Search the scriptures below and ask God to speak to you out of each passage, writing down what He shows you.

1 Samuel 8:10-18 _____

_____

_____

_____

Psalm 11:4-5 _____

_____

_____

_____

Psalm 140:1-3 _____

_____

_____

_____

According to the scriptures you just read, what do you think are the root causes of the violence we see in places like Uganda? _____

_____

_____

What did today's assignment do to make you more aware about this justice issue? _____

_____

_____

_____

Day 2 - Monday

HUMAN TRAFFICKING & EXPLOITATION

"Our lives begin to end the day we become silent about things that matter."

Rev. Martin Luther King Jr, American Civil Rights Leader

DAY 2: HUMAN TRAFFICKING & EXPLOITATION 1

INFORM Slavery was never *completely* abolished. Statistics tell us that there are actually more slaves today than there have ever been. Kevin Bales of Free the Slaves says, "Slavery is what slavery's always been: About one person controlling another person using violence and then exploiting them economically, paying them nothing. That's what slavery's about." Trafficking is defined as the "movement of goods from one area to another for the purpose of buying, selling and trade." Trafficking people is modern day slavery. Victims are forced, defrauded or coerced into labor or sexual exploitation. Many times they are beaten or have their lives and the lives of family threatened if they do not give in to the demands being placed on them.

It is estimated that trafficking generates around $32 billion annually. This makes trafficking in persons the second most lucrative crime in the world. UN Secretary General Kofi Annan stated about slavery that, "despite the efforts of the international community to combat this abhorrent practice, it is still widely prevalent in all its insidious forms, old and new."

The majority of female victims are trafficked into the commercial sex industry. What's more appalling is that it's reported that two children are sold every minute, with over 1.2 million children trafficked annually. In the USA alone, over 100,000 children are forcefully engaged in prostitution or pornography every year! **This has got to STOP!!!**

DAY 2: HUMAN TRAFFICKING & EXPLOITATION 1

ACT It would be easy for those of us in North America to think that this issue is one that is "far away", and that we shouldn't have to worry about it. To believe that would be to ignore a very sad truth; that human trafficking and sexual exploitation are serious problems here as well. As a matter of fact, more than one million women and children are trafficked across international borders every year. In the US alone, between 150,000 and 300,000 children are sold or at risk of being enslaved and sold for sex annually. The sex-slavery industry has become an important revenue source for organized crime because each young girl can earn between $150,000 and $200,000 a year for her pimp.

ASSIGNMENT: *Get a clue!* Today we want you to find out if the local police, sheriff's department, or other professional agencies (hospitals, health organizations, family & social service agencies) are working to tackle trafficking in any way. Contact them and ask specific questions, like:

- Have you ever come across trafficking in this area?
- If you have, we would like to know what was done. If you haven't, what would you do if it was discovered?
- Is there a local Human Trafficking & Exploitation task force in place?
- How can someone who wants to help get involved?

If you aren't able to find cases of trafficking that have happened directly in your area – or your police or other organizations aren't turned onto the issue – it doesn't mean that trafficking isn't going on. It simply means that maybe no one has looked for it yet. Record the responses you get in the area below (names & numbers may come in handy later):

_____

_____

_____

_____

_____

_____

PRAY: For the veil of ignorance to be lifted in our communities, and that operations and organizations involved in human trafficking & exploitation would be discovered and shut down.

DAY 2: HUMAN TRAFFICKING & EXPLOITATION 1

DEBRiEF We have to remember that at the very heart of the issue of human trafficking and exploitation is the root of sin. There are the motivations of selfishness, fear, hatred, lust... the list goes on and on. And we must see this as something that breaks the heart of God and ask Him to cause such sin to break our hearts, too. Take the time to read the scriptures below and ask God to speak to you out of each passage, then write down what He shows you from His Word.

Deuteronomy 22:25-27 _____

_____

_____

_____

Leviticus 19:29 _____

_____

_____

_____

1 Thessalonians 4:3-8 _____

_____

_____

_____

According to the scriptures you just read, what do you think are the root causes of the trafficking & sex trade industry? _____

_____

_____

_____

What did today's task do to make you more aware about this justice issue? _____

_____

_____

_____

Day 3 - Tuesday

"Overcoming poverty is not a gesture of charity. It is an act of justice."

Nelson Mandela, South Africa's 1st Black President

DAY 3: POVERTY 1

INFORM When you read the word "poverty" what do you think of? Do pictures of children with dirty faces flash through your mind? Do you imagine some run down trailer full of people somewhere up in the mountains of rural America? Maybe not many of us picture the homes on our own streets, or have images of our friends come to mind... but the reality is that more Americans are living in poverty than you imagine. The 2011 statistic was that 15.1% of Americans lived below the poverty line. Current "official" unemployment rates in the US are at 10%, but they say the reality is that they are somewhere between 15-20%.

To look up the definition of poverty you would find that it is "the state or condition of having little or no money, goods, or means of support; the condition of being poor..." Some of you reading this right now are squirming because all of this hits home with you... because maybe I'm talking about your family.

There is a mindset here in America that we have nothing to worry about, because compared to the rest of the world we are rich. However, that may not be the case anymore. The year 2009 saw the largest single year increase in the U.S. poverty rate since the U.S. government began calculating poverty figures back in 1959, and according to the Organization for Economic Co-operation and Development, the U.S. poverty rate is now the third worst among the developed nations of the world.

Poverty isn't an issue that is far away anymore. It's not something we only see on TV or when we go with our youth group on a mission trip. Open your eyes because "poor" may not be what you think it is.

DAY 3: POVERTY 1

ACT Something that most of us take for granted is our food. The amount of food that Americans consume each day goes way beyond the needed amount. Most of us eat not just when we need to, but when we are bored or simply when we get a craving for something. Did you know that the variety of what we eat in our meals is considered a luxury in most parts of the world? Today we are hoping that we will help you see that in a very real way.

ASSIGNMENT: *Nothing but RICE!* One food that is the basis of most meals in the rest of the world is RICE. We want you to eat nothing but rice today for all three meals. No meat, no veggies, no desserts, snacks or sweets. Just rice. You'll probably need someone's help with this so make sure your parents know about this assignment! Then, take some time to process what it is that you're feeling throughout the day and record it in this section below.

_____

_____

_____

_____

_____

_____

_____

_____

_____

_____

_____

_____

_____

_____

PRAY: That God would begin to open your eyes and change your perspective to see the poor as He does.

DAY 3: POVERTY 1

DEBRIEF There is a spirit of pride that operates so strongly in most cultures that causes those who have to look down on those who don't. It usually takes a little dose of humility (losing a job, struggling to make ends meet, etc) to give us perspective – but this can also come through God's Word. Romans 12:2 tells us to "renew our minds" and Ephesians 5:26 tells us this is done by a washing that comes from the Word. As you study the scriptures over the next 21 days, let that "bath" take place and allow God to wash away any old mindsets or prejudices.

Read all of **Isaiah 58** and then answer these questions:

What kind of fasting does God desire? _____

_____

_____

_____

What does this passage of scripture teach us about God? _____

_____

_____

_____

_____

What does it teach us about how we should worship God? _____

_____

_____

_____

_____

What did today's task do to make you more aware about this justice issue? _____

_____

_____

_____

_____

Day 4 - Wednesday

"It is poverty to decide that a child must die so that you may live as you wish."

Mother Teresa

DAY 4: ABORTION 1

This is probably the "touchiest" of the justice issues we are taking on, but it MUST be addressed in this generation. Why? Because since 1973, an estimated 54 million babies have been aborted legally in the United States. That is 1/3 of the population that was supposed to be born in the last 38 years. Approximately 24% of all U.S. pregnancies end in abortion. Unbelievably, right now in some demographic groups, there are more babies being legally aborted than are being born alive! But the problem isn't just here at home – worldwide over 46 million babies are killed by abortion every year.

That's one child every two seconds murdered legally, at the hands of a "medical professional."

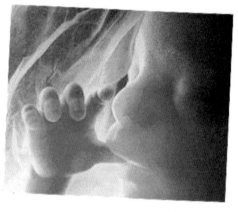

There are many misconceptions clouding the realities of abortion. Many believe that most women are having abortions as a last resort, because their life or the life of their child is in danger or because their pregnancy is a result of rape and even incest. But the reality is that less than 2% of all abortions are performed on women whose lives are in danger or who were raped. The other 98% are elective abortions and are not deemed "medically necessary," but rather are the result of either a mother's choice – or coercion by someone else to make that choice.

Many believe that abortion is perfectly safe and that it doesn't have any negative consequences. However, many mothers and fathers, other family members, former abortion clinic staff – and even several abortion doctors – have testified that abortion hurts women. It can cause severe emotional and physical damage, can be linked to struggles with depression, drug abuse, promiscuity and suicide as well as increase the risk of, or directly cause, infertility and breast cancer.

DAY 4: ABORTION 1

ACT God is a God of great mercy – but He is also very **JUST**. That means He cannot and will not allow evil to go unchecked or unpunished. The verdict against America in the courtroom of Heaven is that the bloodguilt of 50 million babies remains staining our hands and our soil, crying out for justice. The only remedy is for the blood of Jesus to be released over our nation in forgiveness; believing God for His mercy and power in calling her to repentance and healing.

The damage caused to a mother or father as a result of the aborting of their child can literally destroy their lives. Only Jesus' love and forgiveness can mend and heal the wounds of abortion and release someone from the guilt of what they've done. We've been invited into the great honor of intercession with the Son and the Spirit to plead a better blood and see a nation and a generation redeemed and restored!

ASSIGNMENT: *Get a LIFE!* Begin wearing a "LIFE" band from this day forward for the rest of this focus. You can get these from your youth leader or online from **www.bound4life.com**. However, that will take a while to arrive, so if you need to, get a ribbon (maybe from your mom's sewing box or your family's Christmas supplies), a red rubber band, or even just some red tape. By wearing this band we are making a commitment to pray daily for the ending of abortion. God has given the LIFE movement a simple 22-word prayer to replace the one removed from public schools in 1962. It is a powerful point of unity for the movement: *"Jesus, I plead your blood over my sins and the sins of my nation. God, end abortion and send revival to America."* Millions of people are already lifting up this prayer to God day and night for the ending of abortion. Now you can add yourself to that number.

Record below what it is you currently feel about this justice issue:

_____

_____

_____

_____

_____

PRAY: Begin to pray the prayer we just taught you, with conviction!

DAY 4: ABORTION 1

DEBRiEF The thing that you always hear being said in the midst of this issue is that it's a matter of **CHOICE**. Those who say it are right... partially. While they are talking about it being "a woman's right to choose", **the choice that matters has already been made** – by God. No matter the situation under which a child is conceived, God has made the choice of **LIFE** for them! Over the next two weeks we'll look at this more. For now, take some time to really pray as you look at these scriptures and ask the Holy Spirit to speak to you out of His Word. Then write down what He shows you.

Psalm 139:13-16 _____

_____

_____

_____

_____

_____

Genesis 1:27 _____

_____

_____

_____

_____

Isaiah 1:18-20 _____

_____

_____

_____

_____

_____

_____

Day 5 - Thursday

ACCESS TO CLEAN WATER

"When the well is dry, we learn the worth of water."

Benjamin Franklin, American Founding Father

DAY 5: ACCESS TO CLEAN WATER 1

INFORM I've grown up watching TV and seeing those commercials or specials every so often that show starving and hurting people all over the world with their dirty faces and sad looks. Something dawned on me for the first time as I've been doing research for this book and watching similar videos of people from all over the planet... the reason that their faces are always dirty is not because they are lazy and dirty – it's because they don't want to "waste" the water on cleaning their face! That is how precious every single drop of water is to them!

Water. It's running through pipes all around you right now... in the walls, under the ground. You can stand up and walk over to a faucet, turn it on and let it run as long as you want. You can take those nice long hot showers. But, do you ever really think  about the fact that without water life wouldn't exist? We need it to live and thrive. Yet today, nearly one billion people – about one in eight – lack access to clean water. In addition, more than twice that many, 2.5 billion people, don't have access to a toilet.

I've had more than a few people ask me why I've included THIS issue in with the others in this book – basically asking what makes it an injustice. I remind them that part of the definition of an injustice is "when not all people within a society have equal access to the facilities, services or systems within that society". When you think about the fact that the global water and sanitation crisis claims more lives through disease each year than any war claims through guns, you know something must be done! Today's water crisis is not an issue of scarcity, but of access. It's even been said that the ancient Romans had better water quality than half the people alive on the planet today! More people in the world own cell phones than have access to a toilet. Isn't that crazy?

DAY 5: ACCESS TO CLEAN WATER 1

ACT The dictionary defines the word "variety" as "a number of different types of things; an assortment". Here in the US we are so used to having choices with everything... in restaurants, at the movies, buying clothes, in the grocery store. Did you know that there are more than 74 different flavors of Kool-Aid™? Or that Coca Cola™ sells more than 3,500 different types of drinks – and that there are 18 different types of just Coke™ alone? Talk about variety – let's face it, we're spoiled! So, today let's change that a bit.

ASSIGNMENT: *Only water!* Now, we realize that some of you healthy people out there may already do this... but did you know that the average American drinks 1.75 cans of soda per day (making that around 52 a month). Today we challenge you to drink only WATER – no sodas, juice, Kool-Aid™, smoothies, milk, caramel macchiatos... you get the picture. Just water. And go a step further – since most people around the world don't have the luxury of refrigerators or ice, drink your water at room temperature. As you do this, really take some time to think about how blessed you are. Then at the end of the day take some time to process what you felt throughout the day, recording it in this section below.

_____

_____

_____

_____

_____

_____

_____

_____

_____

_____

PRAY: That God would raise up men and women with the knowledge and understanding of how to bring an end to the global water crisis.

DAY 5: ACCESS TO CLEAN WATER 1

DEBRiEF Many people wonder why God would allow drought, famine, and issues like we see take place around the world – but many people don't look to God's Word for the answer. Genesis 3:17-19 tells us that because of Adam's sin, the whole earth (the ground, water, etc.) now has a curse on it as well. The Apostle Paul wrote in Romans 8:18-25 that the earth is "groaning" in an expectation of that day when Christ will come and the curse will be lifted. Keep this in mind as you think about the water crisis issue specifically, and as you read the scriptures below ask yourself what God has done to show mercy to man even in the midst of this curse. Then write down what He shows you from His Word.

Gen 21:14-19 _____

_____

_____

_____

_____

_____

_____

Exodus 3:7-8 _____

_____

_____

_____

_____

Exodus 17:1-6 _____

_____

_____

_____

_____

Day 6 - Friday

HOMELESSNESS

"Human kindness has never weakened the stamina or softened the fiber of a free people. A nation does not have to be cruel to be tough."

Franklin D. Roosevelt
32nd President of the United States

DAY 6: HOMELESSNESS 1

↑NFORM

What would you do if you had no place to live? It's hard to imagine what life would be like without your home, a warm place to sleep, food, your clothes, your phone...your stuff. But many teens just like you don't have to imagine this, because for millions of your peers that's their life.

Some homeless youth are born into poverty and forced onto the streets. Others run away from home. However they end up on the street, 1.6 million young people (between the ages of 12-17) spend at least one night in an emergency shelter or on the street in America each year. The next day, these kids struggle to find a place to eat, bathe and most times to sleep again.

According to *dosomething.org*, 1 in 3 homeless youth are under the age of 18 and the primary causes of homelessness among youth are family conflict or severe economic hardship. Some homeless youth have run away from homes where they were the victims of physical, sexual or emotional abuse. One study reports that more than four in ten youth report being beaten by a caretaker, and a quarter were either sexually abused or feared being sexually abused. Others are running away from alcohol and drug abuse in the home. More than 40% of homeless youth report that one or both of their parents had at some point received treatment for alcohol, drug, or psychological problems. Whatever the reasons, this has become a huge problem that isn't addressed much.

As you can imagine, this issue feeds into another of our issues... human trafficking and exploitation. These vulnerable teens are prime targets for traffickers and many get themselves caught up in a living nightmare.

DAY 6: HOMELESSNESS 1

ACT "I have slept on benches. It makes you feel disgusted because you know it's not where you're supposed to be. You're supposed to be at home with your family." - "Tupac", a homeless teen in Washington, D.C.

ASSIGNMENT: *Hit the Floor!* I really want you to get a little taste of what a homeless teen goes through each night, so tonight lose your comfortable bed and pillow. That's right, grab a blanket and hit the floor (and no music, TV or anything else that you would normally do either!). You may even want to go the extra step and sleep outside on your porch or in your backyard in a large cardboard box - the point is to make it difficult for yourself. If you're doing this with your youth group or a group of friends, you may even want to set up a "homeless camp" at your church or on your college campus for the night to draw attention to this issue in your community.

Record your thoughts throughout the evening in the area below, then come back and record how you feel in the morning, too.

_____

_____

_____

_____

_____

_____

_____

_____

_____

_____

_____

_____

PRAY: That God would give you a heart of compassion for the homeless, and that He would show you what YOU can do to bring about change.

DAY 6: HOMELESSNESS 1

DEBRiEF You may think that homelessness is just another way of talking about poverty, but for many it isn't. Yes, a lot of people end up on the streets because of a financial crisis – but as you've just read, with many teens it is because of something else. Whatever the reason, God wants you to sit up and take notice. He wants you to come to understand His heart for the hurting and to examine this issue yourself to see what it is you can do to make a difference. Take the time to read the scripture portions below and ask God to speak to you, then write down what He shows you from His Word.

Matthew 24:40-45 _____

_____

_____

_____

_____

Psalm 34:17-20 _____

_____

_____

_____

_____

Matthew 6:25-32 _____

_____

_____

_____

_____

According to the scriptures you just read, what do you think God's heart is when it comes to these teens who find themselves on the streets, and what does He want us to do about it? _____

_____

_____

_____

Day 7 - Saturday

THE PERSECUTED CHURCH

"We are not praying that our borders be opened. We are praying that heaven be opened."

The prayer of a church under persecution in Vietnam

DAY 7: THE PERSECUTED CHURCH 1

INFORM When you read that phrase "the persecuted church", what comes to your mind? What do YOU think of when you think of being persecuted for your faith? Maybe it's being shunned by the popular crowd at school, or even mocked by others your age as you worship in a certain way at your church. Though it can be hard to identify the difference between actual persecution and the everyday inconveniences of living in a world hostile towards Christianity, there are some clear defining factors.

Persecution occurs whenever believers are *denied the protection of religious freedom*, prevented from converting to Christianity because of legal or social threats, *physically attacked or killed* because of their faith, *forced to leave their job or home* because of the threat of violence, or *imprisoned and interrogated* for refusing to deny their faith.

It's been reported that there are more Christians being genuinely persecuted in the world today than there have been in all the years combined from the time of Christ until now. Open Doors, a ministry that reaches out to and supports persecuted Christians worldwide, reports that 100 million Christians around the globe are currently suffering persecution for their faith. Most often persecution takes the form of imprisonment, abuse and hostilities. In some cases, however, Christians are asked to face more than scorn, prison, or the loss of health—they are asked to face death. This happens in places we hear about in the news every day. According to a new law in Iran, converts to Christianity face a mandatory death sentence! House churches are monitored by secret police, and members are often arrested, questioned and beaten. In North Korea when Christians are discovered they are sent to deadly labor camps or secretly executed. This isn't 30 or 40 years ago. This is today.

DAY 7: THE PERSECUTED CHURCH 1

ACT Imprisoned. Locked up. Captive. Caged. That is what happens to millions of Christians around the world every year, simply because of their love and devotion to Jesus Christ – something we take for granted. Many of the victims of this injustice do not really get to see the light of day. There is no going to the mall to hang out with friends, no movies, no parks to play in. They are stuck in the same small room or cell all day and night. Some of you may be thinking that wouldn't be so bad, what with your cell phones, internet access, cable, IPod's, video games and more. Well today's assignment will change all of that for you. It's time to have your eyes opened – even if it's just a little.

ASSIGNMENT: *Go to your room!* So that you can get a little bit of a clue as to what these persecuted Christians experience every day, you are going to be locked in your room for the day. You must shut off the cell phone, the TV, the IPods and the computer. And you only get to have one meal today, so let whoever needs to know that you aren't being rebellious... you're just trying to be informed. This will be an uncomfortable time for you, but that will be good. Take some time to process what you're feeling throughout the day and record it in this section below.

_____

_____

_____

_____

_____

_____

_____

_____

_____

PRAY: Very simply, that God would give you a burden to pray for our brothers and sisters in Christ being persecuted around the world.

DAY 7: THE PERSECUTED CHURCH 1

DEBRiEF Knowing how many Christians around the world are being persecuted, it could be easy to get overwhelmed in thinking your prayers won't matter. Do NOT give in to that thinking! In Acts 12 the Apostle Peter was in prison and the church was gathered in secret, praying for his release. When God miraculously set Peter free and he came knocking on the door to THAT very prayer meeting, they didn't believe it was him at the door - in other words, they didn't believe that God would answer their prayers that quickly... but HE DID! God doesn't just hear the things you pray, He answers those prayers, too!

Hebrews 13:1-3 _____

_____

_____

_____

_____

1 Peter 5:8-11 _____

_____

_____

_____

_____

2 Timothy 3:10-13 _____

_____

_____

_____

_____

According to the scriptures you just read, what do you know about persecution of the Church? What do you think are the root causes of this issue? _____

_____

_____

_____

WEEK TWO

A Biblical Response to Global Injustice

"True peace is not merely the absence of tension,
it is the presence of Justice."

Rev. Martin Luther King Jr, American Civil Rights Leader

INSPIRE

WEEK TWO: RETIRED OR RE-FIRED?

I met Bob and Joyce Coder in the late 1990's as I was a youth pastor on staff at a large church in our community. God had healed their marriage, and they had recently surrendered their lives completely to Him. They were an older couple volunteering in the  children's ministry at the time and then God got a hold of their hearts for missions work. Within just a couple of years they started **Wellspring of Life**, sold all they had, moved to Haiti and were drilling wells all over the nation – mountains, valleys, it didn't matter how hard it was to get the rig there, they would do what they could. They stayed in Haiti for 7 years, and during that time drilled **more than 85 wells,** bringing both natural and Living Water to thousands of thirsty people.

Well, you would think that at their age and after having done so much they would come back to Florida and retire, right? Wrong. As they were on a trip to drill a well in Honduras, they were introduced to a small orphanage where the children there captured their hearts. They began to learn that the children were suffering abuse, malnutrition, and being molested by the orphanage's director. After being given custody of the children through legal proceedings, they moved to Honduras, quickly found housing, and began the process of becoming full time caretakers of Fabiola, Rosa, Mauricio, Cesar, Antonio, Angel, and Pedro. That's right, Bob & Joyce (at retirement age) are now the parents to SEVEN young Honduran children! Their story is a constant inspiration to me, and a reminder that "those who know their God shall be strong and do mighty exploits" (Daniel 11:32)! With God, there can be no excuse.

Day 8 - Sunday

"Nothing that you have not given away will ever truly be yours."

CS Lewis
Christian Author & Apologist

DAY 8: POVERTY 2

INFORM If the world were a community of just 100 people, 40 of them would not have shoes! The 300 million children of the world who cannot afford even the simplest pair of shoes are more vulnerable to infection, disease, and cuts – conditions that they most likely already cannot afford to face. In Ethiopia alone, it is estimated that eleven million people are considered to be at risk for Podoconiosis (a disease caused by walking or working barefoot in silica-heavy volcanic soil). It causes extreme swelling, repeated ulcers, and deformity – especially in the legs. This causes a large public health problem in at least ten countries in tropical Africa, Central America and northern India, with upwards of one million people already affected. The solution? Shoes.

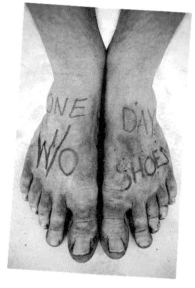

You wouldn't think that something as simple as a pair of shoes could affect the future of a nation, but in reality it does. How? Well, children with shoes are healthier and are more likely to be better students. And since access to education is critical for long-term success in life, it stands to reason that healthy, educated children have a better chance at improving the future of not only their community as they grow up, but their country as well!

Soles4Souls™ and Toms Shoes™ have both started movements in recent years to tackle this issue by holding what they call "barefoot" events. The key with each of these organizations is that what they have *really* done is created a world-wide movement focused on something as simple as putting a pair of shoes on a poor child, while at the same time bringing awareness to this issue. Not just in middle-America, but they are even reaching people in places like Hollywood as well!

DAY 8: POVERTY 2

ACT So, how much do you think about the shoes you own? In the US, on average, girls ages 13-16 may own about 15 pairs of shoes (including sneakers), while females between ages 16-21 have anywhere from 25-40 pairs! The typical guy owns at least 3 pairs of shoes, most have more. So, it can be hard for us to imagine a life without a single pair of shoes... but today you will.

ASSIGNMENT: *No shoes today!* That's right, today it's time to kick off those shoes for the ENTIRE day! It's going to be hard because you're going to have to think this whole day through – because where can you go or not go without shoes? Can you go shopping? To a restaraunt? And how's it going to feel heading to church and being barefoot? When people ask what you're doing, share with them some of what you've learned about this simple injustice. While you're at it, go ahead and snap a pic of your bare feet and post it to any of your online profiles, as this will bring additional attention to the issue. And here is the extra step (no pun intended), why not **DONATE** a pairof new or gently used shoes today to an organization like Soles4Souls? If you're doing this alone or as a family, visit their website for details – or if you're doing this with a group, ask your leader to visit their website to see how your group (or even the whole church or school!) can get involved. Later today take some time to process what it was that you were feeling throughout the day and record it in this section below.

_____

_____

_____

_____

_____

_____

_____

PRAY: That God would show you areas of excess in your life, and what you can do to change that and have an impact in injustices like this.

DAY 8: POVERTY 2

DEBRiEF

What hope do the poor or downtrodden have? Who can they turn to when they have a need? Do the prayers of that broken mom or dad living in a third-world country get answered when they cry out to God for relief? Does He even hear them? The answer is yes, He does. Many times when God hears the cries of the hurting, He will turn and whisper into the heart and ears of His people to bring the answer. We can be like Jonah was at first and ignore His voice because of our own prejudices, or we can be like Jesus and say, "Whatever, wherever, whenever."   Take the time to read the scriptures below and ask God to speak to you out of each passage. Then write down what He shows you from His Word.

Psalm 69:30-33 _____

_____

_____

_____

Psalm 72:12-14 _____

_____

_____

_____

Psalm 107:41-43 _____

_____

_____

_____

What did today's task to do make you more aware about this justice issue? _____

_____

_____

_____

_____

Day 9 - Monday

CHILD SOLDIERS AROUND THE WORLD

"I feel sorry. Why do I feel sorry? Because by the time I could go to school, I am already too old for the beginner's class. I can't dream of going to school anymore because it is too late. I will stay in the army until I die."

A CHILD SOLDIER, Myanmar

INFORM Many armies or rebel groups that use children in combat consider them to be the best soldiers because they are small and nearly invisible when they are moving through the bush. They are fast, nimble, easy to manipulate, very obedient, and are also very brave and undaunted, because they do not fear death. However the main advantage is: they are very "cheap." They don't need any payment and they eat much less than adult soldiers. Both boys and girls are recruited as child soldiers. In countries like El Salvador, Ethiopia, and Uganda, one third of the child soldiers are girls. They are not only used as soldiers, but also as sex slaves for the commanders in countries such as Angola, Sierra Leone and Uganda.

Kids are an easy prey for military recruitment. Manipulating them is easy and they are too young to resist or even to understand the violence they are confronted with. Some of the 300,000 child soldiers in active conflict around the world have joined the army because they are poor. They are often orphans, refugee children or children from extremely poor or broken families. In the army, they find shelter, protection and food – or at least a gun with which to steal the food. Some children have also joined one of the warring parties to take revenge for the death of a family member. But, as we mentioned on Day 1, some tens of thousands of children are recruited under duress and have been abducted by armed forces. In Sierra Leone, an estimated 20,000 children were abducted by rebels of the Revolutionary United Front. In Uganda, more than 30,000 children were abducted by the Lord's Resistance Army. In Congo, all the warring parties recruit children through threats of violence and torture.

DAY 9: CHILD SOLDIERS AROUND THE WORLD 2

ACT

As we mentioned on Day 1, the documentary that brought the plight of these children to the forefront back in 2003 was called "Invisible Children".

ASSIGNMENT: *"I am AWAKE" T-shirt!* Today you are going to bring the attention of your friends to this ongoing issue. Take a white T-shirt (or a light-colored one if you don't have white), get some red fabric paint or a red marker, and draw or paint a big EYE on the front with the words, "I am AWAKE!" When people ask you what this means, tell them about this injustice and let them know you are doing what you can to bring awareness to it – that you aren't asleep to the needs of these children, and that they are not invisible to you. Tell them that they can go to **www.invisiblechildren.com** for more information.

What kind of response or comments did you get from people today?

_____

_____

_____

_____

_____

_____

_____

_____

_____

_____

_____

PRAY: That God would give you a specific burden for the children in one of these countries so that your prayers for this injustice can be FOCUSED, becoming "effectual and fervent" (James 5:16)!

DEBRiEF

The dictionary defines the word "innocent" as "free from moral wrong, pure". That is what we should think when it comes to children, but those that would take them and turn them into killers or sex slaves at such an early age take away their innocence. God has some very specific things to say about those who steel away the innocence of a child, and how those who are a part of His kingdom should be different than the world. Take the time to today to read the scriptures below and ask God to speak to you out of each passage, then write down what He shows you.

Ecclesiastes 9:17-18 _____

_____

_____

_____

_____

Isaiah 59:7-8 _____

_____

_____

_____

_____

Matthew 5:9 _____

_____

_____

_____

_____

What did today's task do to make you more aware about this justice issue? _____

_____

_____

_____

_____

Day 10 - Tuesday

HOMELESSNESS

"Hungry not only for bread - but hungry for love. Naked not only for clothing - but naked for human dignity and respect. Homeless not only for want of a room of bricks - but homeless because of rejection."

Mother Teresa

DAY 10: HOMELESSNESS 2

INFORM I think that when most of us picture a homeless person, we probably think of an older man who may be all ragged and unkempt, missing some teeth, maybe curled up with a bottle on a bench? Man, how wrong can we be? Hopefully some of what you read on the first day we dealt with

this issue started to help change that mindset in you. If it didn't, here are some more statistics from the National Coalition for the Homeless that may open your eyes a bit: the majority of homeless and runaway youth are between the ages of 15 and 17; however 3 out of every 100 runaways are under the age of 10 – and 11 out of 100 are between the ages of 11 and 13. Half of all runaways left home because of a disagreement with a parent or guardian. Homeless youth are up to **ten times more likely** to have or contract HIV than non-homeless youth. One out of ten homeless and runaway females are reportedly pregnant. One out of every seven youth (that's 15% of your peers) will run away from home before their 18th birthday. Each year, approximately 5,000 runaway and homeless youths die from assault, illness and suicide. **A third of all runaways will attempt suicide.** Read that one again.

As I sit here typing this, I keep stopping at that last statistic and my heart is breaking. One third. **That's 528,000 young people** like you every year who have found themselves on the streets... with seemingly no hope, nowhere to turn... hurting, alone, broken... who think that it would be better to end their lives rather than live one more day on the streets. God, have mercy on all of these children! Show us what WE can do to shine some light into their darkened world!!

DAY 18: HOMELESSNESS 2

ACT What would YOU do if you found yourself with no money and no source of income? How would you eat each day or be able to buy the things you'd need to get by? While some homeless have paying jobs, some must seek other methods to make money. One option is called "busking", which is performing tricks, playing music, drawing on the sidewalk, or offering some other form of entertainment in exchange for donations. Begging or panhandling is another option, but it is becoming increasingly illegal in many cities. Despite the stereotype however, not all homeless people panhandle, and not all panhandlers are homeless.

ASSIGNMENT: *What's for Lunch?* So that you know what it's like for at least some of those who are homeless, today your assignment is going to be a humbling one. You are only going to be allowed to eat food for your lunch that you "beg" for. We're not talking about standing on the side of the street or on the corner (that may be too dangerous), but we want you to ask people to help provide your lunch. If you're at school, don't ask your friends or just those that you know – make it a challenge and approach those you don't know. When they ask why you're doing this, share with them some of what you've learned about the injustice of teen homelessness in America.

Come back later and record your thoughts about today's experience.

_____

_____

_____

_____

_____

_____

PRAY: That God would begin to give the Church in your community the knowledge and resources to have a greater impact on homelessness, and that the homeless will be given the revelation of what God says about work and trusting in Him.

DAY 18: HOMELESSNESS 2

DEBRiEF You may think that homelessness is just another way of talking about poverty, but for many homeless it isn't. Yes, a lot of people end up on the streets because of a financial crisis – but as you've just read, with many teens it is because of something else. Whatever the reason, **God wants you to sit up and take notice.** He wants you to come to understand His heart for the hurting, and to examine yourself to see what you can do about **THIS** issue. Take the time to read the scripture portions below and ask God to speak to you, then write down what He shows you from His Word.

Read Mark 14:3-7 and answer the question below:

How do you feel after reading this portion of scripture? _____

_____

_____

_____

_____

Jesus was actually quoting Deuteronomy 15:7. Read it (and continue through verse 11) and then answer these questions:

What does God want our attitude to be towards those who have less than we do? _____

_____

_____

_____

_____

Why do you think it says that "there will always be poor among you"?

_____

_____

_____

_____

Day 11 - Wednesday

HUMAN TRAFFICKING & EXPLOITATION

"Whenever I hear anyone arguing for slavery, I feel a strong impulse to see it tried on him personally."

Abraham Lincoln
16th President of the United States

DAY 11: HUMAN TRAFFICKING & EXPLOITATION 2

INFORM While there are many reasons people are enslaved today, the most common reasons are economic. Globalization has flung wide the doors of economic opportunity, but at a great cost to the millions of impoverished people around the world in developing countries. And while slavery has been *officially* banned by many countries, modern slavery continues *unofficially* beneath other names or titles such as "child soldiers", "debt bondage", and "forced marriage". To make matters worse, many expressions of modern slavery use legal processes as a ruse for bondage, such as adoption and legal prostitution. As you can see, modern slave traders find many ways to exploit a vulnerable people group.

It is important to understand that modern day slavery stems from a variety of other injustices that, taken together, leave multitudes vulnerable to slavery. Poverty, war, and natural disasters all contribute to conditions that leave literally millions of people susceptible to being enslaved. It takes very little for someone in these situations to find themselves suddenly abducted and bound to a life of slavery, even though they are aware of the dangers.

Once enslaved, there is little hope of escape, even in America. Captors are usually extremely powerful, thoroughly intimidating, and capable of brainwashing their captives into a state of "willed" submission, often by frequent beatings and rape. Crime networks easily cross international borders and bribe local police forces to form an inescapable and nearly invisible operation. While it is difficult to accurately pinpoint the number of people enslaved today, experts believe that the number is greater than any other time in human history, and that number most likely exceeds **30 million** people!

DAY 11: HUMAN TRAFFICKING & EXPLOITATION 2

ACT One of the most amazing cultural advances of your lifetime is the invention and development of the internet. It has made access to information more available than ever before through things like Google, and made access to the daily lives of our friends even easier through sites like MySpace and Facebook. However, the internet has also made access to pornography easier and that has helped the human trafficking and sex trade flourish.

ASSIGNMENT: *Get Profiled!* Today you are going to begin to use whatever social media site you are signed up for to bring this issue to the forefront. Have someone take a creative picture of you that you can post as your "profile pic" for the rest of your "Extreme Days". Print out or make a sign that you can hold in your picture that will bring awareness to this issue – things like:

- Slavery Still Exists
- Real Men Don't Buy Girls
- "Love146.org", "ExodusCry.org" or "theA21campaign.org"

If your youth or college group is doing this together, see if your leaders would set up a "photo booth" area where these photos can be taken in your youth or meeting room. Take pics with your friends too, and upload them together to really cause a stir in your community about this issue. At the end of the day, come back and share some of your thoughts about this issue and maybe some other ideas it's given you to make an impact in this justice issue:

_____

_____

_____

_____

_____

_____

PRAY: That laws would be put into place in your community and state that don't put the weight of punishment on the teens caught up in this injustice, but on the traffickers and the ones who abuse them.

DAY 11: HUMAN TRAFFICKING & EXPLOITATION 2

DEBRIEF

Interestingly, when many people talk about trafficking today, they call it the "new slavery." But there is really little that is "new" about it, with the exception of how modern technological advances make it easier than ever for traffickers to traffic, and for those that take part and those that make money in it to exploit and profit. Actually trafficking in persons is an ancient problem and the examples of the practice are seen in the earliest chapters of the Bible. The story of Joseph is one of the earliest accounts of human trafficking found in the Bible. Read the following passage and then describe how this was human trafficking.

Genesis 37:13-28_____

_____

_____

_____

_____

Now take the time to read Genesis 39 and describe the things that happened to Joseph that could be considered slavery and exploitation.

_____

_____

_____

_____

_____

Finally, read Genesis 41:41-57 and describe the end result of Joseph's struggles and tell how a similar hope can be had by those found in a slavery or exploitation situation today: _____

_____

_____

_____

_____

_____

Day 12 - Thursday

THE PERSECUTED CHURCH

"We don't pray to be better Christians, but that we may be the only kind of Christians God means us to be; Christ-like Christians; that is, Christians who will bear willingly the cross for God's glory."

From a note smuggled from the underground church in Communist Romania

DAY 12: THE PERSECUTED CHURCH 2

INFORM

Brad Phillips of the **Persecution Project Foundation** tells the story of an 8-year old boy who was kidnapped in Darfur, Sudan, then taken North to be sold as a slave. One day he snuck away to go to a church, and while he was gone some of the sheep and camels he was supposed to be watching got away. When his master discovered what was missing, he first beat the boy then told him that he would do to him what was done to Jesus. He took him and **nailed his hands and then knees to a board**.

Eventually that boy was purchased, rescued and brought back to southern Sudan. His village welcomed him back and then gave him the new name "Joseph". As a teen he responded to the Gospel message and gave his life to Jesus and was filled with a new joy. He now speaks about his old master who tortured him with words of **forgiveness and peace**. Joseph's story is just one out of 100 million just like his.

Think about something for a moment: Joseph is part of the family of God... meaning that he is your brother in Christ. Every persecuted believer in the world is part of a huge family that we belong to. In Genesis when God asked Cain where his brother Abel was, Cain responds with, "Am I my brother's keeper?" The rest of the Bible answers that question for us – "Yes, we are." In Hebrew tradition, "tzedakah" (justice) is the term used to describe acts of caring and philanthropy. It is what must be done, even when we have to push past our initial desire not to or when we think that we lack the resources to do it. It even extends to those who may not "deserve" our help, or to those whose actions got them into this situation that now demands our rescue. It is what God expects us to do... to be our brother's keeper, standing faithfully with our family being persecuted around the globe. It's time to activate our compassion.

DAY 12: THE PERSECUTED CHURCH 2

ACT Romans 10:17 says, "So then faith comes by hearing, and hearing by the word of God." It has been estimated that 50% of the world has never even seen one verse of Scripture and that 75% of the Christians of the world do not even own a Bible – especially those in countries where they are being persecuted for their faith. How can this world be reached with such a lack of access to the Word of God? The world is starved for Bibles while we in America take ours for granted. According to a Gallup poll taken way back in 2000, 92% of U.S. households have at least 1 Bible, and most Christian homes have around 5 (and that doesn't mean they're reading them, just that they own them). In our home we have at least 15! I recently read a story about a church in India who were blessed enough to have 1 Bible for the entire congregation. Do you know how they got Bibles for the rest of the church? They would divide their one Bible among the members – 20 pages to one family, 20 pages to another. The family would then take the pages home and copy them and then swap until they had a complete Bible! Now THAT is having a hunger and love for the Word of God!

ASSIGNMENT: *Just ONE page!* Can you imagine trying to live your life as a Christian without access to ALL of God's Word? Do you think you could survive on just ONE book of the Bible? What about just one CHAPTER? Well, that is what you'll have for the next 3 days... just one chapter of the Bible to focus on. **You are only allowed to read from Hebrews 11, nothing else**. To make sure you don't get tempted, put your Bible away and look in the Appendix in the back of this manual where Hebrews 11 is provided for you. You may also want to pray about making a donation to one of the ministries that gets Bibles into the hands of those around the world who don't have them. Since it can cost **as little as $2 per Bible** to do that, why not cut the sweets or fast food for a couple days and put that money aside for this cause? Most gourmet coffee drinks cost at least $4. Think about that – you could provide **TWO** Bibles a week to those who need it, by cutting out just **ONE** drink!

DAY 12: THE PERSECUTED CHURCH 2

DEBRiEF Since you only have Hebrews 11 to read through the next couple of days, I want you to really allow God to speak to you through THAT chapter about these justice causes. What do you see in this chapter about Christians being persectured for their faith? Write down what God has shown you from His Word.

_____

_____

_____

_____

_____

_____

_____

_____

_____

_____

After reading these verses, what do you now think of the assumption that most Christians in our culture make that says nothing "bad" or "difficult" will ever happen to you if you give your life to Christ?

_____

_____

_____

_____

PRAY: That God would give YOU the same boldness and courage in your faith that those being persecuted in other countries have. And, that God would increase that burden you asked for last week.

Day 13 - Friday

"I've noticed that everyone who is for abortion is already born."

Ronald Reagan, 40th President of the United States

DAY 13: ABORTION 2

INFORM One of the things you have probably heard said by women who stand on the side of abortion is, "Well, it's my body to do with what I want." This would be true if a baby wasn't involved! At conception, every unborn child has their own unique DNA-sequence. This DNA-sequence is the blueprint their body will use to form, grow and function for the rest of their life. At the moment of conception, this DNA already contains details including hair and eye color, fingerprints, and even the child's gender.

A developing child has a beating heart by 3 weeks. At the same time their brain, spinal cord and nervous system are already forming. At one month the muscles are forming, and arms, legs, ears and eyes can be seen. By 5 weeks, brain waves can be detected and recorded and by 8 weeks, every organ is present. By 12 weeks the child is blinking their eyes and sucking their thumb. The child sleeps and awakens and has their own unique set of fingerprints, now completely formed. He or she can grab anything that is put into the palm of the hand. The child is breathing amniotic fluid, strengthening the developing lungs.

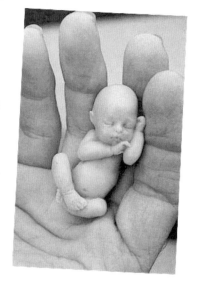

Approximately 80% of abortions are performed during the first trimester of pregnancy – at or before 12 weeks – while all of what we just described is happening. That baby's life can be terminated for $300, or about the price of an Xbox 360 or I-Phone.

First trimester abortions are legal in all 50 states, in many places up to 24 weeks, and in some places up to the time of natural birth. An entire generation has been fooled into believing that abortion is the best choice for many families in crisis – that it solves problems and causes no additional distress to those involved. This is deception on both a natural and spiritual level, because Scripture says that LIFE is in the blood, and that the justice of God demands that innocent bloodshed be avenged.

DAY 13: ABORTION 2

ACT Unborn children that are aborted have been denied their God-given right to LIFE based merely upon the inferiority of their size, their developmental stage and their ability to speak for or defend themselves. Every human life is precious – no matter what the situation surrounding how the baby was conceived, whether it will be born with a handicap, or if that baby's birth will make life uncomfortable for the parents. Every baby conceived has been placed in the womb by God Himself, full of potential and promise. Acts 17:26 tells us that God has chosen not only WHEN in history we are to be born, but WHERE as well – that mother and womb.

ASSIGNMENT: *Don't drop it!* To show you how precious the life of a baby should be, why not get a little creative today? Your assignment is to carry an egg around with you all day, making sure that you are careful not to drop it. We actually challenge you to go a step further... hollow it out (YouTube can show you how) and commit to not putting it down even once throughout the day. It may mean having to switch from hand to hand or getting a little creative, but you can do it! WHY be **THIS** specific? Because the majority of abortions done are done for the sake of convenience. So, don't just set the egg down when it gets hard or if you're sick of carrying it around – just like we want people to stay committed when they get pregnant. Come back at the end of the day and write about your experiences.

_____
_____
_____
_____
_____
_____
_____

PRAY: That adoption would get greater attention so that those considering abortion can see that there is another option in their crisis.

DAY 13: ABORTION 2

DEBRiEF "So the mother who is thinking of abortion, should be helped to love - that is, to give until it hurts her plans, or her free time, to respect the life of her child. The father of that child, whoever he is, must also give until it hurts. By abortion, the mother does not learn to love, but kills even her own child to solve her problems. And by abortion, the father is told that he does not have to take any responsibility at all for the child he has brought into the world... Any country that accepts abortion is not teaching the people to love, but to use any violence to get what they want." *(from Mother Teresa's speech at the US National Prayer Breakfast - February 4, 1994)*

Psalm 127:3... "Children are a heritage from the Lord, offspring a reward from him." _____

_____

_____

Galatians 1:15-16... "But when God, who set me apart from my mother's womb and called me by his grace, was pleased to reveal his Son in me so that I might preach him among the Gentiles, my immediate response was not to consult any human being." _____

_____

_____

_____

Job 10:8-12... "Your hands shaped me and made me. Will you now turn and destroy me? Remember that you molded me like clay. Will you now turn me to dust again? Did you not pour me out like milk and curdle me like cheese, clothe me with skin and flesh and knit me together with bones and sinews? You gave me life and showed me kindness, and in your providence watched over my spirit." _____

_____

_____

_____

(Now take a look at Hebrews 11 and see what God speaks to you from there)

Day 14 - Saturday

ACCESS TO CLEAN WATER

"Thousands have lived without love, not one without water."

W.H. Auden, American Poet

INFORM

How long is your typical shower? 10 minutes? Maybe 15 or 20? How would you feel if I told you that someone who takes a 5-minute shower uses more water than a typical person in a developing country slum uses in a whole day? How about a bath? Your bathtub probably holds about 40 gallons of water. Compare that to the 8 gallons someone in a slum MAY get to use in a day or the 2.6 gallons for those who have no access to running water. According to the US Geological Survey, the average American uses from 80-100 gallons of water in a day. With just turning your faucet on it pours out 1.5 gallons per minute. That is a LOT of water!

One of the things we said last week about the water issue is that it's not really a matter of **NOT** having it... it's a matter of not having **ACCESS** to it. Less than 1% of the world's fresh water (or about 0.007% of all water on earth) is readily accessible for direct human use. So people living in the slums often pay 5-10 times more per liter of water than wealthy people because the plumbing or infrastructure isn't in place.

Now, have you ever said to yourself, "If I didn't have to do THIS, then I'd have more time to do THAT!" Well, think of what life is like for the millions of women and children who spend several hours a day collecting water from distant, often polluted sources. Polluted because these people will bathe, dump waste into, and wash their clothes in the same water they draw to drink from. In just one day, more than 200 million hours of women's time is consumed for the most basic of human needs — collecting water for domestic use. According to Gary White, co-founder of Water.org, this lost productivity is greater than the combined number of hours worked in a week by all the employees at Wal*Mart, UPS, McDonald's, IBM, Target, and Kroger combined.

DAY 14: ACCESS TO CLEAN WATER 2

ACT

When I was 18 years old, I got on a plane and headed to Paraguay, South America to spend a year as a missionary helping to plant a church. For half of my time there I lived with a few other guys in the little town we were trying to reach, in a house that had not one, but TWO wells. Funny thing, that the pumps on both of our wells broke and became too expensive to fix, so we resorted to having to draw water each day for cooking, cleaning, and anything else requiring water. Now that wouldn't have been so bad if I hadn't gotten sick and had to run out to the well about 15 times a day just to flush the toilet! Needless to say, I learned to appreciate life "back home" with constant running water any time I needed it. Especially considering that the average distance a woman in Africa and Asia walks to collect water is 6 km (that is 3.75 miles)!

ASSIGNMENT: *Take a Walk for Your Water!* Today you may need to enlist the help of your youth pastor, parents, or a friend with a car. You'll need to take two empty one-gallon milk or juice containers and rinse them out. Then fill them up with good, clean, safe drinking water. When this is done, figure out a location that is ONE mile from your house. Then, take your two gallons of water and drop them off at that location, go back to your house (or church, etc) and then walk BACK to get the water, then carry it back home. Got that? Now, you may be thinking, "Man, that's pretty far!" Well, it's not so bad compared to the almost 8 miles round trip that they make for water in Asia or Africa! If it feels like the water is getting heavy, just think about those women and children who carry multiple gallons at a time on their heads. According to DropInTheBucket.org, the weight of water that women in Asia and Africa carry on their heads is equivalent to the maximum baggage weight allowed by airlines of 20 kg, or 44lbs!

Now, when you get back home **DO NOT DO ANYTHING WITH YOUR WATER**. We want you to put it someplace out of the way, because you'll be using it on Monday for that day's assignment.

PRAY: That God would bring finances into those ministries and organizations doing a valid work to bring water to these crisis areas .

DAY 14: ACCESS TO CLEAN WATER 2

DEBRiEF

There is a theme that runs throughout the whole Bible and it compares our need for God with our natural thirst for water. Think about that. There are many times we get thirsty (after eating something salty, working out, on a hot day)... but think about someone who is desparate for even just a sip of water. If God uses this comparison, then what does that tell us? It says that He knows that water is VITAL to our human existance. Consider this as you look at the scriptures below. Write down what God speaks to you.

John 4:10-15... "Jesus answered her, 'If you knew the gift of God and who it is that asks you for a drink, you would have asked him and he would have given you living water.' 'Sir,' the woman said, 'you have nothing to draw with and the well is deep. Where can you get this living water? Are you greater than our father Jacob, who gave us the well and drank from it himself, as did also his sons and his livestock?' Jesus answered, 'Everyone who drinks this water will be thirsty again, but whoever drinks the water I give them will never thirst. Indeed, the water I give them will become in them a spring of water welling up to eternal life.' The woman said to him, 'Sir, give me this water so that I won't get thirsty and have to keep coming here to draw water.'" _____

_____
_____
_____
_____

Revelation 21:6... "He said to me: "It is done. I am the Alpha and the Omega, the Beginning and the End. To the thirsty I will give water without cost from the spring of the water of life." _____

_____
_____
_____

Now turn to Hebrews 11. What do you see about our need to depend upon God for everything, even our existance? _____

_____
_____
_____
_____
_____

A Biblical Response to Global Injustice

"Faith is not even worthy of the name until it erupts into action."

Catharine Marshall, Christian Author

ÎNSPÎRE

WEEK THREE: LIGHT YOUR CANDLE

In 1989, Laszlo Tokes was the pastor of the small Hungarian Reformed Church in Timisoara, Romania. He preached the Word of God boldly and did not fear the communist regime that was in power. The government didn't like this and did several things to get him to stop, but he wouldn't and his church grew to over 5,000 members! Fed up, the police went to his home to arrest him – but they were stopped cold by hundreds of people from several churches who had surrounded the home in his defense, many staying late into the night. A young Baptist college student named Daniel Gavra had brought a box of candles. He took one out, lit it, and passed it along, doing this until there was a sea of faces lit by the glow. Pastor Tokes recalls that being a turning point in his life, as looking out his window his religious prejudices evaporated. Here were members of the Body of Christ laying aside their denominational differences to stand in his defense.

Finally the government had had enough, and they ordered the police to break through the crowd and bring Pastor Tokes to the central police station. The crowds grew larger as they now went and surrounded this building, holding vigil once again late into the night. And again, there was Daniel and his box of candles. Now the religious protest had turned into a full-scale protest against the communist government. The next morning, troops were brought in and soldiers were ordered to fire into the crowd. Hundreds were shot. Young Daniel felt a searing pain as his leg was blown off, but the people of Timisoara stood bravely against the barrage of bullets. Their example inspired the whole nation to rise up and within days they had overthrown the communist government.

Daniel celebrated in the hospital where he was learning to walk with crutches. His pastor came to see him and offered his sympathy, but Daniel wasn't looking for it. "Pastor, I don't mind so much the loss of a leg," he said. "After all, it was I who lit the first candle." The candle that lit up an entire nation.

Day 15 - Sunday

THE PERSECUTED CHURCH

"If you are not willing to die for what is in the Bible, you should not give money for Bibles. Because if you give, we will smuggle more Bibles. And if we smuggle more Bibles, there will be more martyrs."

Pastor Richard Wurmbrand
Author of Tortured for Christ

INFORM

One of the biggest injustices in the world is that there are Christians living in countries where they can not worship God freely – whether in group settings or even in private homes. I think that in our culture, this is probably one of the biggest things we take for granted as Christians. Is your relationship with Jesus so important to you, that if access to a worship service wasn't a choice of waking up on time, but whether you were willing to lay your life down, that you'd still be there?

This is some of what was reported from around the world in the week following November 1st, 2010: In Uzbekistan 20 police raided a private home during a house church, the Believers were beaten and threatened, Bibles were taken from the children, and the leaders were arrested. In Kusar, Azerbaijan, police raided a Baptist house church, threatened the Christians and arrested 4 of the leaders. In a village in Northern India, two church buildings and 400 homes of Christians were raized and burnt, leaving 1000 families homeless (including children, babies, pregnant woman, and the severly ill). And in Baghdad, Iraq, in what was called "the most lethal attack on Christians there in 7 years", Islamic militants stormed a church where 100 people were worshiping. They began firing at worshipers, and a leader was pushed to ground. When he pleaded for the gunmen to spare others, his body was riddled with bullets. The gunmen then held others hostage for 4 hrs, until the Iraqi army attacked. The gun battle led to the death of 58 Christians. When rescue workers rushed in, they found blood smeared on walls and scraps of flesh on the ground. The group that took responsibility later made the statement, "All Christian centers, leaders, and followers are legitimate targets for us wherever we can reach them."

DAY 15: THE PERSECUTED CHURCH 3

ACT Within just a week of those tragedies happening, a Christian leader from Central Asia came to the US for the first time and visited a large church in Birmingham, Alabama. When he walked into the church's sanctuary it's reported that he said, "This is like heaven to have a room this large where you can gather together and sing praises, without having terrorists outside waiting to storm in and slit your throat." Wow! Can you imagine the pressure? Most of us only worry about not getting stuck in the church lobby or parking lot too long so we can beat the crowd to our favorite restaurant. We're hoping that today's assignment will maybe bring a little perspective to that.

ASSIGNMENT: *Secret Church Service!* If your group or church is doing Extreme Days together, talk to your youth pastor or pastor about doing this special service to draw awareness to the plight of the persecuted church around the world. The goal is to strip away all of our cultural flash – the lights, the loud music, the video screens, the choirs, no coffee shop in the lobby that day, etc. Worship would be simple and very quieted down (only a guitar or no instrument at all), and the preaching would be straight from the Word of God... no skits, videos, props or anything else that usually is found in many American church services these days. As part of this special service, celebrate communion together, but do it in the simplest of ways. No fancy trays being passed – instead encourage the people to come forward and get a simple piece of bread and dip it into a shared cup, or pass the bread and cup around. Why communion? Because this simple act of worship unites us with our brothers and sisters in Christ around the world.

If you aren't able to participate in something like this at your church, go ahead and do this at home with your family and maybe even some invited friends or neighbors. Use the same guidelines laid out as above and do all that you can to make this time special. Whichever way you do this, make sure to spend time praying for the persecuted Church.

PRAY: That God would bless converts to Christianity in these crisis nations. Ask God to enable them to be instruments of blessing (salt), transformation (yeast), and truth (light) in their communities (Matthew 5:13-16).

DAY 15: THE PERSECUTED CHURCH 3

DEBRiEF You've had a lot to take in today. Hopefully what this day has done is brought you to the very basis of your relationship with Jesus by asking how committed you would be to worship Him if it were extremely difficult to do so. Persecution is actually what caused the Gospel to be taken from the confinement of one city (Jerusalem) to the openess of the entire known world. As Christians were first arrested then killed, others scattered and took the message of Christ with them. The first of those who gave their life for Jesus was a young man named Stephen. After you read his story below, record your thoughts about his courage, his words, and his death. Ask God to really speak to you from Stephen's story,   then write down what He speaks to you.

Acts 6:8-8:1 _____

_____

_____

_____

_____

_____

_____

Ephesians 6:18-20 _____

_____

_____

_____

_____

Revelation 12:10-11 _____

_____

_____

_____

_____

Please take a look at tomorrow's ACT right now, it takes some planning!

Day 16 - Monday

ACCESS TO CLEAN WATER

"When you're thirsty, it's too late to think about digging a well."

Japanese Proverb

DAY 16: ACCESS TO CLEAN WATER 3

INFORM Remember that the big issue for many families around the world is the lack of ACCESS to clean water. Currently there are 884 million people globally that lack access to safe water supplies; that's approximately one out of every eight people. Think about this for a moment... not having access to clean water leads to disease and even death. It's been reported that **HALF** of the world's hospitalizations are due to water-related diseases. **HALF!** That is a pretty staggering figure, when you consider that they wouldn't be sick if those people simply had **ACCESS** to the water that is many times already there flowing in the ground beneath their feet.

One of the biggest groups that are affected by this injustice are children. Lack of access to clean water and sanitation kills children at a rate equivalent to a jumbo jet crashing every four hours. Of the 3.575 million people that die each year from water-related disease, 1.4 million of them are children – that's every 20 seconds that a child dies from a water-related disease!

What can be done to stop this number from climbing each year? What can **YOU** do to help halt this injustice? **FIRST**, what you are doing now... become aware. **SECOND**, connect with a ministry or organization that is already there, on the ground and drilling wells to bring water to those who need it. Many groups I researched in writing this show that they can bring someone access to clean water for life **for as little as a gift of $25**! That is LESS than the cost of most video games we buy and waste time with ... less than a night out for two at the movies... less than the cost of a new skirt or pair of jeans... less than a magazine subscription. The point is, we spend money on things that don't matter that could go to something that does... saving someone's life.

DAY 16: ACCESS TO CLEAN WATER 3

ACT Remember how I told you about my year in South America, and all that water I had to draw from a well? Thinking back now, I remember how creative I had to get so that I didn't have to keep running out to pull up yet another bucket of water to use. We would go out there faithfully every morning to bathe ourselves – rain or shine, hot or cold (and man, did it get cold some days!). There were times we so wanted a hot shower or bath, that we'd heat up several pans of water and pour them into a big laundry basin in our bathroom and use that as "the world's smallest bathtub", all to make life feel even a little "normal"! The thing I do remember is how we figured out how to use a minimal amount of water for even some of the toughest jobs. I'm hoping that today's assignment will maybe bring you some of that awareness, too.

ASSIGNMENT: *It's a TWO-GALLON day!* So, today is the day you get to do something with the 2 gallons of water that you walked for on Saturday. It will be a BIG challenge, as you **ONLY** get to use those **2 gallons** for **ALL** of your water needs today! That means for bathing, drinking, brushing your teeth – even cooking if possible (that would take some planning with your parents). Yeah, this is going to be hard, but we think you can do it – and it will help you learn to appreciate all that wonderful water that you get to use each and every day. Come back throughout the day and write down how much you used (and for what), to keep things in perspective:

_____
_____
_____
_____
_____
_____
_____
_____

PRAY: That God would call more full-time, trained workers into this area of missions. And pray that those He calls, that He will provide for.

DAY 16: ACCESS TO CLEAN WATER 3

DEBRiEF This issue really is a huge one, and it could be overwhelming to think that we may never see it tackled in our lifetime. The thing to keep in perspective is that we serve a merciful God, full of compassion and love for those He has created. He wants that water to flow to those people more than you do. He knows where it is, and what it takes to bring it to the surface... and He has called people into service to be the ones who can or will do this. Whether they be missionaries, vounteers, government employees, or whomever – God always chooses to work through **PEOPLE** to get things done, just like you'll see in the first scriptures below. Sometimes it's a practical work and sometimes it's a miraculous one. Maybe He is calling **YOU** to be one of those people working in this injustice. Ask God to really speak to you from Stephen's story, then write down what He speaks to you.

Exodus 17:5-7 _____

_____

_____

_____

_____

_____

Luke 9:12-16 _____

_____

_____

_____

_____

_____

John 6:48-51 _____

_____

_____

_____

_____

Day 17 - Tuesday

HOMELESSNESS

"People who are homeless are not social inadequates.
They are people without homes."

Sheila McKechnie
European Political Leader/Activist

DAY 17: HOMELESSNESS 3

INFORM When Jesus makes the remark in Matthew 26:11 that "you always have the poor with you" He was quoting Deuteronomy 15:11, "since there will never cease to be poor people on the earth, I therefore command you, 'open your hand to the poor and needy in your land.'" In Mark 14:7 Jesus reaffirms the command found in Deuteronomy when He finishes the sentence with a reminder that "they can always do good to the poor".

The world will always have poor people, and not simply because of their financial needs. No, the world will always have poor people only because in every society and in any age, there will always be those less capable of providing for themselves. Maybe it would be due to some physical or mental limitation, or because something happened in their life that caused them to need a hand to move on. Now, from a Biblical perspective, a just society should seek to govern its economic affairs in ways that prevent structural inequality and provide the resources needed to those less able to fend for themselves. But, even if we did reach that level of economic justice, the poor will still be with us.

You would be surprised at some of the people in the Bible who today would be considered "homeless". Jacob was the patriarch of Israel, yet he had a pillow of stone and he wandered about for a time trying to figure out how to get his substance. Joseph was thrown out of his home by his brothers and sold as a slave. David was driven from his home and lived in caves. John the Baptist had what was considered vile clothing – AND he ate bugs and honey. We don't know who might be homeless out there and we don't know what God's plan for one of them could be. But what if **YOU** are part of that plan?

DAY 17: HOMELESSNESS 3

ACT OK, to drive home this issue you've already given up the comfort of sleeping in your bed for a night, and then you had to beg for your lunch – hopefully both assignments gave you a taste of what the homeless might face each day. Now we want you to experience something else that they deal with – not being able to have a fresh set of clothes to change into!

ASSIGNMENT: *Wear it Again!* You know the clothes that you wore yesterday – the ones that are probably sitting in a pile on your bedroom floor? Or maybe they are in the corner of your bathroom, or already at the bottom of the dirty clothes basket in the laundry room. Well, go get them because today you get to wear them again – that's right, all of them, right down to your socks and underwear. Now if you REALLY want to get extreme, don't take a shower or brush your teeth (because most on the streets don't have access to these luxuries – especially those living in other countries). When people ask why you're doing this, take the opportunity to share with them about this injustice.

Come back later and record your thoughts about today's experience.

_____
_____
_____
_____
_____
_____
_____
_____
_____
_____
_____
_____

PRAY: Ask God to infuse mothers and fathers whose families are in or facing a homeless crisis with HOPE that there is a way through this time.

DAY 17: HOMELESSNESS 3

DEBRIEF When we work with the homeless, we always need to be careful and prayerful for safety's sake. Back in the days of the Great Depression, people would take strangers into their home and feed them and let them stay with them. However, ungodliness was not as rampant as it is today. In Biblical accounts when people saw beggars, they knew who they were. The beggars were well known to the community. Someone would bring them to the temple to beg and the people knew that these beggars had no ability or capacity to work for themselves. They were usually blind or crippled, and they didn't have Social Services to fall back on. Sadly, we can't deal with homelessness like they did. Today you must be careful because of the danger of being taken advantage of in our society. So, we must first test the Spirit. Take the time to read the scripture portions below and ask God to speak to you, then write down what it is that He shows you from His Word.

Read Matthew 6:25-34 and answer the question below:

How do you feel after reading this portion of scripture? _____

_____

_____

_____

Now read James 2:1-13 and answer these questions:

How do we show favortism to those who are "better off" in our time?

_____

_____

_____

Why do you think that James tells us showing favortism is called a sin?

_____

_____

_____

_____

Day 18 - Wednesday

"Poverty is the worst form of violence."

Mahatma Gandhi

DAY 18: POVERTY 3

INFORM What would you do with just half? Half the Starbucks, half the movies, half the fast food, half the TV watching, half the clothes... half the house? Yeah, you read that right. Half the **HOUSE**.

That's what the Salwen family in Atlanta, Georgia asked after an encounter at a red light one day. While waiting at a traffic light, then 14-year-old Hannah saw a black Mercedes coupe on one side and a homeless man begging for food on the other. "Dad, if that man had a less nice car, that man there could have a meal," Hannah commented. Her dad's response was, "Yes, but if we didn't have such a nice car that man could have a meal." This sank in a little more deeply than he'd intended and by dinnertime, Hannah was all worked up. She said that she didn't want to be a family that just talked about doing good. "What do you want to do?" her mom responded. "Sell our house?" And Hannah said, "Yeah! That is exactly what I want to do." And that is what they DID do!

Over the next year, the family of four met every Sunday morning to discuss what to do with half of the money from selling their 6500 sq ft home (they downsized to a home half its size). They had committed to give at least $800,000 from the sale to whatever project they would settle on – which ended up being an organization that works to end hunger and start micro-business in Ghana, West Africa. The experience so impacted their lives that they wrote a book, *The Power of Half*, and now travel the country challenging others to consider what the power of giving up HALF of something in their life can do!

DAY 18: POVERTY 3

ACT Now, most of you probably don't live in a home as big as Hannah's was – or if you suggested selling your home and giving half the money away, your parents would probably think you're crazy. BUT, all of us do have SOMETHING that we could give up half of for a good cause, right? Maybe it's only getting half as many coffees this week, or spending half as much as you normally do on things like fast food or iTunes. Maybe you'd be willing to give half of your shoes or clothes to a local homeless ministry or women's shelter. Or maybe your family or roommates would be open to donating half of your canned and dry goods to your church's food pantry or a local feeding program. Another idea is to give up half the time you would spend watching TV, surfing the web, or playing video games and donate that time to visiting a nursing home or local orphanage. How about those of you with really long hair... would you be willing to give half of its length to something like "Locks of Love"?

ASSIGNMENT: *Cut it in HALF!* Now it's time to figure out what YOUR "half" is going to be. Really make this challenging, so that this assignment will really have a lasting impact on you. If it's something that you end up saving money on, put that money in your "rescue" jar. Then, take some time to journal about how you came to your decision and how this has and will impact you in this section below.

_____
_____
_____
_____
_____
_____
_____
_____

PRAY: Ask God to break the power of the spirit of poverty over your community. Ask Him to remove the stigma that comes with this spirit.

DAY 18: POVERTY 3

DEBRiEF When we are in the middle of tragedy or hard times, hearing someone say something as simple as, "I know how you feel" can be as

Proverbs 25:11 says, "Like apples of gold in settings of silver is a word spoken in right circumstances" (NASB). It's not only good because we know someone is there, but it is good because we know that someone who understands is there!

Read all of **Psalm 102** and then answer these questions:

What is it that is causing the writer distress? _____

_____

_____

_____

What is it that brings the writer hope? _____

_____

_____

_____

Now read **Matthew 26:6-13** and then answer these questions:

Was what this woman did really a waste – why or why not? _____

_____

_____

_____

_____

How is it that when we do something extravagant or extreme, that it can be an act of worship to the Lord? _____

_____

_____

_____

_____

_____

Day 19 - Thursday

HUMAN TRAFFICKING & EXPLOITATION

"He who passively accepts evil is as much involved in it as he who helps to perpetrate it. He who accepts evil without protesting against it is really cooperating with it."

Rev. Martin Luther King Jr
American Civil Rights Leader

DAY 19: HUMAN TRAFFICKING & EXPLOITATION 3

iNFORM

In 2002, the co-founders of the organization "Love 146" traveled to Southeast Asia on an exploratory trip to determine how they could serve in the fight against child sex trafficking. In one experience, a couple of their co-founders were taken undercover with investigators to a brothel, where they witnessed children being sold for sex. This was their experience and the story that changed our lives.

"We found ourselves standing shoulder to shoulder with predators in a small room, looking at little girls through a pane of glass. All of the girls wore red dresses with a number pinned to their dress for identification. They sat, blankly watching cartoons on TV. They were vacant, shells of what a child should be. There was no light in their eyes, no life left. Their light had been taken from them. These children...raped each night... seven, ten, fifteen times every night. They were so young. Thirteen, eleven... it was hard to tell. Sorrow covered their faces with nothingness. Except one girl. One girl who wouldn't watch the cartoons. Her number was 146. She was looking beyond the glass. She was staring out at us, with a piercing gaze. There was still fight left in her eyes. There was still life left in this girl...

"...All of these emotions begin to wreck you. Break you. It is agony. It is aching. It is grief. It is sorrow. The reaction is intuitive, instinctive. It is visceral. It releases a wailing cry inside of you. It elicits gut-level indignation. It is unbearable. I remember wanting to break through the glass. To take her away from that place. To scoop up as many of them as I could into my arms. To take all of them away. I wanted to break through the glass to tell her to keep fighting. To not give up. To tell her that we were coming for her..."

"Because we went in as part of an ongoing, undercover investigation on this particular brothel, we were unable to immediately respond. Evidence had to be collected in order to bring about a raid, and eventually justice on those running the brothel. It is an immensely difficult problem when an immediate response cannot address an emergency. Sometime later, there was a raid on this brothel and children were rescued. But the girl who wore #146 was no longer there. We do not know what happened to her, but we will never forget her. She changed the course of all of our lives." - Rob Morris, President and Co-founder

DAY 19: HUMAN TRAFFICKING & EXPLOITATION 3

ACT In the Bible, Jesus tells the story of a man who discovers a treasure in a field, and then goes and sells all that he has to buy that field so that the treasure can be his. In our culture we are constantly assigning value to the things and even people around us. We think of what brings us joy in light of how much it will cost us, then how much time it will take to work to pay for that. The average teenager doesn't make much more in an hour than it costs to buy a double mocha frappacino at the local coffee shop – but we'll run right out to buy it, sometimes daily. What is really hard to imagine is that for as little as the cost of that cup of iced coffee and whipped cream, it will buy you an hour of sexual perversion with a child in some places in the world.

ASSIGNMENT: *Declare yourself "SOLD".* Today we want you to take out a simple piece of masking tape, white duct tape, or even a piece of cardboard paper. In big red letters write the word "**SOLD**" on it and attach it on your shirt, wrist or some other obvious place. When people ask you why it's there, tell them that you are trying to bring awareness to the issue of human trafficking & exploitation in the world. Share with them some of the statistics you have learned, or go to our website and download the simple pamphlets that you can pass out. At the end of the day, come back and record your experiences here:

_____

_____

_____

_____

_____

_____

_____

_____

PRAY: Ask God to help the rescued victims of this injustice, that as they return home that they would not be shunned by their families. Pray that God would equip the Church to help in these times of transition.

DAY 19: HUMAN TRAFFICKING & EXPLOITATION 3

DEBRIEF The question we need to ask now is, "What is the **RIGHT** response to the injustice of human trafficking and exploitation?" To answer that, we have to turn to the Bible for examples.

First, read these two chapters from Genesis and then describe if the response was right or not.

Genesis 34_____

_____

_____

_____

Genesis 38_____

_____

_____

_____

Now, read Jesus' encounter with a prostitute in John 4:1-42 and describe how He responded to her situation: _____

_____

_____

_____

_____

Finally, read Jesus' encounter with another prostitute in John 8:1-11 and describe how He responded to her situation: _____

_____

_____

_____

_____

After reading Jesus' response to this sin, what should our motivations be in offering hope to those bound by this sin? _____

_____

_____

_____

_____

Day 20 - Friday

CHILD SOLDIERS AROUND THE WORLD

"They gave me pills that made me crazy. When the craziness got in my head, I beat people on their heads and hurt them until they bled. When the craziness got out of my head I felt guilty. If I remembered the person I went to them and apologized. If they did not accept my apology, I felt bad."

A 13-year old former child soldier from Liberia, West Africa

INFORM

UNICEF (the United Nations Children's Fund, which provides long-term humanitarian and developmental assistance to children and mothers in developing countries) reports that the LRA has abducted children as young as 5 but mostly between the ages of 8 and 16, often after killing their parents in front of them. The young "recruits" are then

forced to march to southern Sudan. Those who can't carry their loads or keep pace with the others are killed. Those who attempt escape are severely punished. Girls are routinely raped.

Ugandans may be at highest risk of abduction, but children in other nations have plenty to fear as well. In Bhutan, Burundi, Myanmar, El Salvador, Ethiopia and Mozambique, children have even been kidnapped while at school. The "Child Soldiers Report 2008" notes that the same is true in Bangladesh and Pakistan. Warlords in Afghanistan and Angola have a system in which they demand that villages each hand over a certain number of youths. Those villages that don't oblige are attacked.

Those who are rescued from combat, or who survive until the conflict's conclusion, face an enormous challenge in trying to return to normal civilian life. In the past it was just the immediate physical needs that were met, but now there is much being done to help meet their emotional and psychological needs as well. The goal here is to see the stop of this practice of involving children in these armed conflicts. But only with wide-spread awareness and mobilized action will something be done to end this injustice and send these kids home. See the "**Get Connected**" section at the end of this manual to see what more you can do to help end this injustice in our lifetime.

ACT There are many ministries and organizations that are tirelessly at work around the world combating this injustice. They realized somewhere along the way that it's not enough to sit back and talk about (or throw money at) a problem and think that it will simply go away. We must get involved and be willing to go the extra step if God asks it of us.

ASSIGNMENT: *The Auction Block!* Today you get the opportunity to "rescue" that thing that you had to surrender on Day 1. Hopefully over the last 3 weeks you've been collecting spare change (or even larger donations) from your friends and family. Tonight invite as many people to your home (or if your youth group is doing this, to the church) for a special time together. At this gathering you will have the opportunity to exchange the money for your item, but you will also get the chance to share with those you've invited about this injustice and encourage them to get more involved. If you have the ability, show the full "Invisible Children" film or the 30-minute stories "The Rescue: Full" or "Kony 2012" (which are found at vimeo.com in the "Invisible Children" section), or "An Unconventional War" by the Sentinel Group. Do your best to have information, posters, fliers, etc. out on the table that also show the 6 other justice issues that you have been learning about over the last 3 weeks. Now, I know that giving up your item and the "rescue" today is tied to the child soldier injustice, but maybe one of the other 6 injustices has been the one that has really captured your heart. Let the Holy Spirit lead you, and take the money that YOU have collected in your "rescue" jar and send it to that organization that is doing the most to help bring an end to that injustice. Or, maybe as a youth group you've decided to pool your money together to have an even greater impact on one or two of the injustice issues. You may think that the amount you've collected is insignificant and won't matter much in taking on such a huge issue. Don't think that... because every little bit counts. Yes, it's one drop in the bucket... but you know what? Every bucket is full of many little drops of water just like yours.

DEBRIEF

What you did tonight in "rescuing" your item doesn't even come close to the reality of what children go through around the world each and every day. Each one is waiting to be rescued from the darkness they are in and hoping to one day go home and be restored to their families... and to one day live in a place of peace. God blesses those who are all about peace – see what His Word has to say today about this subject, and write down what He speaks to you.

Isaiah 59:12-19 _____

_____

_____

_____

Matthew 5:9 _____

_____

_____

_____

1 Corinthians 7:21-24 _____

_____

_____

_____

What has God shown you about this justice issue over the past three weeks, and what do you think you can do to get more involved?

_____

_____

_____

_____

_____

PRAY: Ask God to give these children HOPE for a beautiful future that God has already planned out for them... that they would not give up and think they can't return home and live a "normal" life once again.

Day 21 - Saturday

"We must not be surprised when we hear of murders, killings, of wars, or of hatred... If a mother can kill her own child, what is left but for us to kill each other?"

Mother Teresa

DAY 21: ABORTION 3

ÎNFORM

If countless testimonies report that abortion hurts women, and medical and scientific evidence reveal that it ends the life of a real and fully-human being, why then does it remain legal? The answer is disturbingly simple – **it is a multi-billion dollar industry.** The single largest abortion-provider alone generates a billion dollars in annual revenue. One third of those billion dollars **comes from taxpayer money,** and a large portion of that is funneled back into the political machines that help ensure that the industry remains publicly funded and unmanaged by the government. These incentives provide a powerful motivation and drive to defend the right to offer and perform abortions without restriction.

What's crazy about it all is that families in crisis are looking for help from an industry which profits from their misfortune. That's like buying medicine from a store that is selling you the poisoned milk you are getting sick from in the first place! Then these families are duped into believing that the industry itself is committed to compassionately helping them find a sure solution from their problems. In reality, abortion has become just another thing to be "sold" so that someone can make more money.

Those whose lives have been impacted by abortion carry the guilt and shame of their sin while all the time being told by society and the law that they've done nothing wrong. Many retreat into years of silent torment, unable to recover from the devastation. But still others have found freedom, forgiveness, life and healing in the atoning blood of Jesus Christ. There is an entire generation to be healed and restored from the deception of abortion and God has invited us to make intercession on their behalf. You never know when you may come across or sit next to a "silent sufferer," waiting to hear of the love and forgiveness of Jesus Christ that was shown to us on the cross.

DAY 21: ABORTION 3

ACT The solution to this injustice is a supernatural one. In all of history there is found only One Man, whose innocent bloodshed has the power to release a man or woman from both the temporal and eternal consequences of their sin, and the troubles that wreak havoc on a fallen world. Yet somehow, we have bought into a lie that we can sacrifice our children at this man-made altar of convenience and atonement and work our own deliverance and salvation, apart from the blood of Jesus Christ. This is the foolishness of man, and the end is death.

ASSIGNMENT: *Do a Silent Siege!* A "silent siege" is where we silently stand in the gap on behalf of our nation and build up a wall of prayer (Ezekiel 22:30). This strategy was given to a young man in the Bound4Life movement in a dream from the Lord. He saw young people standing in front of the Supreme Court building with red tape across their mouths with the word "LIFE" written on it. As they were already on their way to Washington DC to pray for the upcoming elections, they went to the Supreme Court building and simply did what he saw in that dream. The media has taken hold of this image and spread it everywhere and it's become a phenomenon that catches the eyes and hearts of the world. So, when we make a stand outside of a courthouse or an abortion facility, our stand is for life, mercy, and justice.

When **LIFE** is written on a piece of red tape and placed over our mouths, we are identifying with the silent cries of the preborn—those who have no voice to defend themselves. This stand is **NOT** a protest; what it IS though, is a SILENT PRAYER MEETING. We make our appeal to the Judge of the earth and ask Him for speedy justice to be released (Luke 18:7-8). It's also a plea for God to subpoena the conscience of the nation. There are no signs being waved, no yelling and screaming. It is simply PRAYER.

Go with your youth group, family or a group of friends and spend two hours today doing this. Find a local abortion clinic or city or county court house that you can stand in front of. Face the building and silently pray with red LIFE tape on your mouths. Make sure to not block sidewalks or interfere with anyone coming or going. Again, this is not a protest, but simply a silent prayer meeting, asking God to move on behalf of the unborn and the lives affected by this injustice. For more information or tips, visit the Bound4Life website.

DAY 21: ABORTION 3

DEBRiEF You've come through you're last assignment, and we know this one may have been a tough one. Ezekiel 22:30 says, "I looked for a man among them who would build up the wall and stand before me in the gap on behalf of the land so I would not have to destroy it, but I found none." That is a HUGE thing for God to not find even ONE who would intercede and pray for the nation – but today that was not the case! You and your family or friends have "built up a wall" and "stood in the gap" on behalf of the unborn and those who would be tempted to abort them! Now take some time to look into God's Word and let him speak to you, then write down your thoughts.

Proverbs 31:8 _____

_____

_____

_____

Luke 18:1-8 _____

_____

_____

_____

_____

What did you feel as you stood up silently for the unborn today, and what impact do you think you had? _____

_____

_____

_____

_____

PRAY: That God would give you a heart of compassion and understanding for those considering an abortion, and the words of love to say in order to help them.

INSPIRE

AFTERWARD: AND NOW WHAT?

"One day we will have to stand before the God of history and we will talk in terms of things we've done. Yes, we will be able to say we built gargantuan bridges to span the seas, we built gigantic buildings to kiss the skies. Yes, we made our submarines to penetrate oceanic depths. We brought into being many other things with our scientific and technological power. It seems that I can hear the God of history saying, 'That was not enough! But I was hungry, and ye fed me not. I was naked, and ye clothed me not. I was devoid of a decent sanitary house to live in, and ye provided no shelter for me. And consequently, you cannot enter the kingdom of greatness. If ye do it unto the least of these, my brethren, ye do it unto me.' That's the question facing America today."

Martin Luther King, Jr. from his sermon at the National Cathedral, Washington D.C., on March 31st, 1968.

The past 21 days for you have been different, haven't they? Maybe you stretched yourself more than you ever have. Maybe for the first time in your life you started to look at the world around you and the issues we all face with different eyes. Maybe you've never realized before how God looks at the cares of this world, or what His Word says about how much He really does care. As I said at the beginning of this book, we have to realize that the Gospel doesn't stop with salvation – the change that takes place in our life when we invite God in should be the power that then compels us to confront such darkness in the world. Simply put, we have got to start making a difference.

In Luke 19 Jesus tells a parable about a rich man who, before traveling away to a far country, gives each of his servants a different measure of money. Along with the money he gives them one command... "Occupy until I return." In the original Greek, that word means "to do business" or "to get to work". Now, every parable that Jesus told was because He had something that He wanted to teach them – and us. So, what was Jesus telling them? In essence He was saying, "You know what guys? I'm putting a lot into your hands… and I'm going away, but I will be back. While I'm gone you have got to get to work and give me a return for what I'm investing in you." And I believe that is what He says to us. We live in a day and time where we have SO MUCH at our fingertips. We can jump on a plane and be on the other side of the world in a matter of hours! That trip would have taken several months even one hundred years ago. And regardless of your family's financial picture, even the poorest of us here in America are rich compared to the majority of the world. Plainly said, we have been given much. God has put a lot into our hands, and now He expects a return on His investment.

So, where do you go from here? What do you do next? Well, start with prayer. Ask God to lead you as you consider your next step. Then, why not take a look once again at those one or two justice issues that captured your heart over these past three weeks? In the pages following this I've listed out the ministries and organizations that I've looked into that are already doing a good work to combat the evil of those seven injustices. Go to their websites and research for yourself what they are doing. Watch the videos and read their stories, and let their testimonies sink in and cause those seeds of change inside of you to grow. Then get involved – support those already involved in the work, and pray about getting more involved yourself.

The worst thing that you could do is be like the servant in Jesus' parable that simply took what he'd been given and did nothing with it. He was rebuked because there was not even the littlest return on the man's investment. Over the last 21 days something has been put into your hands too – information. You now can never say that you don't know what is going on around you… you can't claim ignorance. What you CAN do is be about the Father's business. You can love and serve the hurting around you, and in doing that you live out your love for God.

APPENDIX

Additional Resources and Information

HEBREWS 11 *(NIV – New International Version)*

Faith in Action

[1] Now faith is confidence in what we hope for and assurance about what we do not see. [2] This is what the ancients were commended for.

[3] By faith we understand that the universe was formed at God's command, so that what is seen was not made out of what was visible.

[4] By faith Abel brought God a better offering than Cain did. By faith he was commended as righteous, when God spoke well of his offerings. And by faith Abel still speaks, even though he is dead.

[5] By faith Enoch was taken from this life, so that he did not experience death: "He could not be found, because God had taken him away."For before he was taken, he was commended as one who pleased God. [6] And without faith it is impossible to please God, because anyone who comes to him must believe that he exists and that he rewards those who earnestly seek him.

[7] By faith Noah, when warned about things not yet seen, in holy fear built an ark to save his family. By his faith he condemned the world and became heir of the righteousness that is in keeping with faith.

[8] By faith Abraham, when called to go to a place he would later receive as his inheritance, obeyed and went, even though he did not know where he was going. [9] By faith he made his home in the promised land like a stranger in a foreign country; he lived in tents, as did Isaac and Jacob, who were heirs with him of the same promise. [10] For he was looking forward to the city with foundations, whose architect and builder is God. [11] And by faith even Sarah, who was past childbearing age, was enabled to bear children because she considered him faithful who had made the promise. [12] And so from this one man, and he as good as dead, came descendants as numerous as the stars in the sky and as countless as the sand on the seashore.

[13] All these people were still living by faith when they died. They did not receive the things promised; they only saw them and welcomed them from a distance, admitting that they were foreigners and strangers on earth. [14] People who say such things show that they are looking for a country of their own. [15] If they had been thinking of the country they had left, they would have had opportunity to return. [16] Instead, they were longing for a better country—a heavenly one. Therefore God is not ashamed to be called their God, for he has prepared a city for them.

[17] By faith Abraham, when God tested him, offered Isaac as a sacrifice. He who had embraced the promises was about to sacrifice his one and only son, [18] even though God had said to him, "It is through Isaac that your offspring will be reckoned." [19] Abraham reasoned that God could even raise the dead, and so in a manner of speaking he did receive Isaac back from death.

[20] By faith Isaac blessed Jacob and Esau in regard to their future.

²¹ By faith Jacob, when he was dying, blessed each of Joseph's sons, and worshiped as he leaned on the top of his staff.

²² By faith Joseph, when his end was near, spoke about the exodus of the Israelites from Egypt and gave instructions concerning the burial of his bones.

²³ By faith Moses' parents hid him for three months after he was born, because they saw he was no ordinary child, and they were not afraid of the king's edict.

²⁴ By faith Moses, when he had grown up, refused to be known as the son of Pharaoh's daughter. ²⁵ He chose to be mistreated along with the people of God rather than to enjoy the fleeting pleasures of sin. ²⁶ He regarded disgrace for the sake of Christ as of greater value than the treasures of Egypt, because he was looking ahead to his reward. ²⁷ By faith he left Egypt, not fearing the king's anger; he persevered because he saw him who is invisible. ²⁸ By faith he kept the Passover and the application of blood, so that the destroyer of the firstborn would not touch the firstborn of Israel.

²⁹ By faith the people passed through the Red Sea as on dry land; but when the Egyptians tried to do so, they were drowned.

³⁰ By faith the walls of Jericho fell, after the army had marched around them for seven days.

³¹ By faith the prostitute Rahab, because she welcomed the spies, was not killed with those who were disobedient.

³² And what more shall I say? I do not have time to tell about Gideon, Barak, Samson and Jephthah, about David and Samuel and the prophets, ³³ who through faith conquered kingdoms, administered justice, and gained what was promised; who shut the mouths of lions, ³⁴ quenched the fury of the flames, and escaped the edge of the sword; whose weakness was turned to strength; and who became powerful in battle and routed foreign armies. ³⁵ Women received back their dead, raised to life again. There were others who were tortured, refusing to be released so that they might gain an even better resurrection. ³⁶ Some faced jeers and flogging, and even chains and imprisonment. ³⁷ They were put to death by stoning; they were sawed in two; they were killed by the sword. They went about in sheepskins and goatskins, destitute, persecuted and mistreated— ³⁸ the world was not worthy of them. They wandered in deserts and mountains, living in caves and in holes in the ground.

³⁹ These were all commended for their faith, yet none of them received what had been promised, ⁴⁰ since God had planned something better for us so that only together with us would they be made perfect.

GET CONNECTED

The ministries and organizations listed below are already doing a good work in each of the areas we've touched on in *The Justice Revolution*. A lot of the research and statistics shared throughout the pages of this book were gleaned from their websites or printed materials. I encourage you to contact and partner with them to help see their work continue, to learn more about these justice issues, and to see what you can do to get personally involved. By no means are these the only organizations working in each area, but they are ones that I know are already doing a good work, and they are worth taking a long look at.

POVERTY

Operation Blessing at www.operationblessing.org
The Salvation Army at www.thesalvationarmy.org
The Salwen Family at www.thepowerofhalf.com
The Hunger Project at www.thp.org
Soles4Souls at www.giveshoes.org

THE PERSECUTED CHURCH

Voice of the Martyrs at www.persecution.com
International Christian Concern at www.persecution.org
Intl Day of Prayer for the Persecuted Church at
www.persecutedchurch.org
Christian Freedom International at www.christianfreedom.org
Persecution Project Foundation at www.persecutionproject.org
Providing Bibles for the World at www.billionbibles.org

HUMAN TRAFFICKING & EXPLOITATION

Love 146 at www.love146.org
Make Way Partners at www.makewaypartners.org
Exodus Cry International at www.exoduscry.org
The Sold Project at www.thesoldproject.org
Stop the Traffik at www.stopthetraffik.org
The A-21 Campaign at www.thea21campaign.org
The Magdalene Project at www.themagprojectnow.com

ABORTION

Bound 4 Life at www.bound4life.org
Operation Rescue at www.operationrescue.org
ProWoman/ProLife at www.prowomanprolife.org
Priests for Life at www.priestsforlife.org

ACCESS TO CLEAN WATER

Wellspring of Life at www.wellspringoflife.org
Blood Water Mission at www.bloodwatermission.com
The 100 Wells Campaign at www.100wellscampaign.com
Water for All at www.waterforall.org
US Agency for International Development at www.usaid.gov

CHILD SOLDIERS AROUND THE WORLD

Invisible Children at www.invisiblechildren.org
Enough Project at www.enoughproject.org
Coalition to Stop the Use of Child Soldiers at www.child-soldiers.org
World Vision at www.worldvision.org

HOMELESSNESS

Covenant House Ministries at www.covenanthouse.org
Family Promise at www.familypromise.org
International Street Kids Outreach at www.internationalstreetkids.com
Stand Up for Kids at www.standupforkids.org
The Salvation Army at www.thesalvationarmy.org

ANOTHER RESOURCE: THE 40 DAY REVOLUTION

The 40 Day Revolution is a prayer and evangelism strategy for teens that has PROVEN results! Since it's writing close to 1,000,000 teens and adults committed themselves to seeing TRANSFORMATION take place on their campuses, at their workplace, and in their homes.

In 1998 a small group of youth pastors got together to hammer out what would become the four elements that make up the foundation of *The 40 Day Revolution*: prayer & fasting, blessing, serving, and telling the Gospel story. They started there and came up with 40 simple tasks that could be done over a 40-day period that would share the love of God in a practical way.

Each of those 40 simple tasks was designed to do two things, 1) to show the one doing it how EASY it is to share the love of God with people, and 2) to get the one being blessed or served to ask WHY it is being done for them. This gives the one doing it the opportunity to share the Gospel, pray for that person, or simply invite them to church. The testimonies have been overwhelming as THOUSANDS have come to know Christ, schools have been turned upside down and opened completely up to the Gospel, and MIRACLES have taken place.

The impact of this strategy has been reported by CNN, CBN, and many local new agencies.

For more information on how to start *The 40 Day Revolution* on your own or with a group, visit www.OperationLightForce.com

A Justice United™ Conference

PROJECT 330

Targeting Human Injustice, Modern Slavery, and Global Poverty

MUSIC BY

Jesus Culture
Hillsong United
Planet Shakers
United Pursuit

Featuring speakers
from around the world...

Register Now!

Philadelphia, PA - Sept 26-28, 2012
Liacouras Center at Temple University

JusticeUnited™

justiceunited.org
facebook.com/Justice-United
Twitter - @justiceunited1

NOTES

NOTES

NOTES